Faith, Hope and Love

*Interfaith Engagement
as Practical Theology*

Ray Gaston

scm press

Published in 2017 by SCM Press
Editorial office
3rd Floor, Invicta House,
108–114 Golden Lane,
London EC1Y OTG, UK

www.scmpress.co.uk

SCM Press is an imprint of Hymns Ancient & Modern Ltd
(a registered charity)

Hymns Ancient & Modern® is a registered trademark of
Hymns Ancient & Modern Ltd
13A Hellesdon Park Road, Norwich,
Norfolk NR6 5DR, UK

British Library Cataloguing in Publication data

A catalogue record for this book is available
from the British Library

978 0 334 05459 7

Typeset by Manila Typesetting Company
Printed and bound by
CPI Group (UK) Ltd

Contents

Acknowledgement

This book is rooted in two particular contexts: my time as a Parish Priest in Leeds and secondly as a theological educator in Birmingham. In Leeds I'd like to thank particularly the Muslim communities in Hyde Park Leeds at the Makkah Masjid and the Grand Mosque as well as the Ahlul Bayt Islamic Centre for their hospitality and welcome in the years between 1999–2007. In Birmingham, I'd like to thank our Muslim neighbours in Sparkhill who welcomed us into the area that became our home for eight years and the Methodist Church which for four years was my spiritual home as I preached on Christian discipleship in a multi faith world Sunday after Sunday and during the week explored the same subject in classes and workshops. I'm grateful for the enthusiastic participation of students at Queens Foundation for Ecumenical Theological Education who took my courses for the 9 years I taught as Tutor in Inter Faith Engagement, particularly those who took the undergraduate module Christianity and Inter Faith Engagement that provided much of the material for the first chapter and for the stimulating exploration of the MA module *Theology in Dialogue* and to my co-tutor on that module Richard Sudworth for the dialogue we sought to model and the discussions it encouraged.

I'd also like to thank folk in our current home of Wolverhampton: Clive Gregory the Bishop of Wolverhampton who allowed me time in my new role as Bishop's Interfaith Enabler to complete this book and for the encouragement from my new brothers and sisters in Christ at St Chad and St Mark where I am now Team Vicar. Finally, but most importantly, I'd like to thank my beloved soul friend Annie Heppenstall, my wife, for her constant support. A writer of 10 books on Christian spirituality, she is much more accomplished at producing a book than I, and was an experienced source of encouragement and challenge when I thought the task too great.

Introduction

This book seeks to respond to four areas of concern in interfaith engagement. First, it considers that we are in a context in which our multifaith reality can no longer be ignored. Even in those places in the UK where the presence of people of other faith traditions is minimal, the reality of global communications and the internet at least means that people are increasingly aware that there are many alternatives to Christianity and that the much-vaunted secularization thesis is seriously open to question. We live in a world of what might be termed 'multifaith consciousness', where access to resources of the world's different faith traditions is at our fingertips and interest in and the continued growth of religion a reality, despite the decline of Western Christianity. We are also in a country where the continued privileging of Christianity in the public square is increasingly questioned.[1]

Second, Christian theological reflection on this reality is also at a crossroads. For several years the theology of religions has been framed within the typology, presented most clearly in 1983 by Alan Race, of exclusivism, inclusivism and pluralism.[2] This model of approach to other faith traditions emphasized Christian understandings of the other's salvific destiny – are *they* saved. Similarly, missiological reflections often centred on learning about the other to approach *them* apologetically or in open proselytization. In theology of religions, several approaches have developed that seek to postpone or bracket the salvific question. Comparative theology seeks to do theology in an awareness of other religions, deeply engaging with their texts, practices and philosophies to help inform Christian theological reflection.[3] Particularism seeks to assert the necessity for any engagement with other faith traditions to be rooted in the Christian narrative, and calls for Christian theological reflection on other religions to be engaged in the particularity of a Trinitarian understanding of God.[4] Others have sought to reassert in the face of this challenge to the typology a new pluralism that moves on from the typology in its classical formation and incorporates aspects of the comparativist and particularist agendas into pluralist theological reflection.[5]

Third, the interfaith movement has changed. The organizations and networks of the 1970s – often set up by liberal Christians concerned to welcome and help communicate to wider society the religions of those who came from the former colonies to work and live in the UK in the postwar period – have largely run their course. Often created to resist prejudice and misunderstanding, these groups played an important role in the struggle in the 1970s and 1980s against racism and in developing friendships between people of different faiths.[6] However, in many cases they were the concern of a small minority of practitioners and were sometimes detached from the traditions they sought to represent. Increased government interest in religion – first with what some saw as New Labour's concern to establish a new multifaith religious establishment through the funding of multifaith forums,[7] second through forms of community organizing in the larger multifaith conurbations,[8] third through the development of the Near Neighbours programme[9] under Conservative rule – have led to new forms of civic interfaith engagement that has often been led by people of other faith communities and has different concerns from those of the older interfaith networks and are sometimes led by local authority or central-government funding. Under the influence of the civic models and what some have referred to as the particularist turn, interfaith engagement has become less the exclusive domain of the liberal interfaith practitioner. Scriptural reasoning, although still a minority pursuit, has engaged more conservative forms of particularly the Christian, Muslim and Jewish traditions in a form of engagement that emphasizes the particularity of each tradition and the prioritizing of the interpretation of their Scripture to contemporary issues.[10]

Finally, all this has developed with the continued backdrop of 9/11, 7/7 and the 'war on terror'. There has also been increased interest in the growing presence of Muslims in Europe through various forms of migration. As will be shown, this interest has been largely malevolent in its intent, with increasing prejudice in wider society promoted by strands of the media and through the discourse of the 'war on terror', increased surveillance and monitoring of the Muslim community by the state.[11]

In response to these four developments I argue that, first, in the light of growing 'multifaith consciousness', Christian discipleship can no longer ignore this reality. More importantly, in a time of church decline, interfaith engagement needs to be brought centre stage, not relegated further to the margins. My argument is that our increased multifaith reality is an opportunity for growth, not through proselytization and the seeking of conversions from other faith traditions (although people will inevitably not feel confined to their religion of birth in an increasingly pluralist society), but because encounter with other faiths and interfaith engagement can be a 'means of grace' by which the Christian disciple is renewed and encouraged in her own faith and the Church can rediscover its vocation in a 'post-Constantinian' context in which Christianity's centuries-long privileged position is thankfully undermined.

Second, theological exploration needs to move beyond the old contestations established in the theology-of-religions typology. The focus on the other's salvific destiny needs to be replaced with a focus on the impact of interfaith engagement on the theological self-understanding of the disciple and the Christian community in light of this engagement. A dialogical theology that emphasizes the necessity of intra-Christian engagement to enable the fullest and truest witness in our multifaith context is essential. Also, new contestations between particularism and pluralism need to be challenged. This book's argument is that a more holistic theological engagement with our multifaith reality can be enhanced by a practical theological turn in our reflection on interfaith engagement; and its methodology emphasizes that.[12]

Third, my concentration in this book is not so much on traditional interfaith practitioners, either of the old liberal form or the new civic type (although these do feature), but on a more radical engagement, sometimes in contexts in which the interfaith engagement is not seen as such. Charismatics meeting Muslims and Jews on the Walk of Reconciliation, Christian Peace activists marching with Muslim neighbours against the invasion of Iraq, Christians in local contexts joining with Muslim neighbours to protect their towns and cities from Islamophobic demonstrations – these are the particular contexts in which this book reflects on Christian self-understanding in light of an activism that brings the Christian community into a different kind of contact and dialogue with people of other faiths than is often possible with official interfaith practices.

Fourth, the book unashamedly prioritizes the engagement with Islam, given the context mentioned above of growing prejudice and surveillance of the Muslim community in this country and elsewhere in the European and US contexts. The history of Christian–Muslim engagement is not one that we can be proud of and it is also the premise of this book that in a post-Constantinian world, engagement with Islam can help us dethrone the imperial Christianity that still resides in our hearts. The challenge of engagement with Islam for the Euro-American Christian is, I would maintain, an opportunity for growth and renewal in an age of spiritual and theological malaise in our Church.

The book is divided into two parts. In Part 1, I explore the method and practice of a practical theology of interfaith engagement, drawing on two contexts. The first is my time as a tutor and theological educator in the Church at Queen's Foundation for Theological Education (2008–17) and the Birmingham Methodist District (2008–12), where I was responsible for teaching interfaith engagement with ordinands and other students and helping Methodists in the West Midlands explore their multifaith context. Chapter 1 comes almost totally out of this work and focuses on how I draw on the methodology of theological reflection to enable creative engagement with contemporary multifaith consciousness in ordinands and congregants. The second context is my time as an Anglican parish priest in Hyde Park, Leeds between 1999 and 2007, where engagement with the local Muslim community post 9/11 and 7/7 was a significant part of my ministry.[13] Chapter 2 begins to draw these two strands together as I move from a focus on a pedagogy in Chapter 1 that draws on methods of theological reflection, to a focus in Chapter 2 on the post-9/11 context of my own engagement, drawing on philosophical and hermeneutical approaches that enhance an autoethnographic exploration of my deepening engagement with Islam at this time. These two chapters draw on the primary material of students, congregants and my own experiences and bring them into conversation with theoretical perspectives that enable a critique of contemporary debates in theology of religions and its offshoots from the perspective of a practical theology of interfaith engagement. Chapter 3 takes this exploration further, focusing on an approach that draws on the Peace Church tradition and Wesleyan understandings of the 'way of salvation' to explore how a commitment to Christological non-violence might have an impact on interfaith engagement and how drawing on Wesley we may see our engagement as a 'means of grace' enabling the repentance, conversion and sanctification of the Christian in dialogue. Once again through autoethnographic exploration, my own experience and the experience of the community among whom I ministered in Leeds is analysed, but this time alongside 'case studies', both contemporary and historical, of Christian engagement with Islam in the context of the Crusades. This chapter concludes by proposing a practical theology of radical renewal through engagement with other faiths in our contemporary context.

In Part 2 my reflections move specifically to an exploration of contemporary questions related to Islamophobia and multiculturalism that are rooted in my own practical engagement with these questions as a community resident and activist in South Birmingham, where I was involved in campaigns to get the police to take English Defence League (EDL) Islamophobic violence seriously[14] and in a campaign to remove 'spy cams'[15] erected in our locality to monitor the Muslim community as part of the 'war on terror'. Chapter 4 explores three case studies of Christian involvement in community responses to the Islamophobic EDL in Tower Hamlets, Bradford and Luton, and concludes that to enhance such an engagement a theological affirmation of multiculturalism is required. In my final chapter I begin this process, drawing on sociologists from Muslim backgrounds exploring multiculturalism and Muslim consciousness, a virtues approach to dialogue and biblical and Qur'anic exegesis combined with stories of personal encounter to promote a spiritual theology for multiculturalism rooted in Paul's 'Hymn to Love' in 1 Corinthians 13.

This book draws on work undertaken in the last nine years. Chapters 1 and 2 first saw life as a paper produced for a conference in September 2013 on the typology 30 years after the publication of Alan Race's *Christians and Religious Pluralism*. That paper ended up as a chapter, *Twenty-First Century Theologies of Religions: Retrospection and Future Prospects*, in the book of the conference papers, edited by Elizabeth Harries, Paul Hedges and Shanthikumar Hettiarachchi and published by Brill-Rodopi in 2016 as 'The Typology and Theological Education: Towards a Practical Theology of Interfaith Engagement'. The version here is a considerable expansion of that chapter with additional material, including some drawn from work done during my year of study at the Centre for Muslim–Christian Relations in Birmingham between 2007 and 2008. Chapter 3 began life as a paper at the University of Winchester conference on 'Interfaith and Social Change: Engagements from the Margins' in September 2010. I returned to the initial paper and expanded it for the Anne Spencer Memorial Lecture at the University of Bristol in February 2015 entitled 'Interfaith Encounter as Christian Spiritual Practice'. I am particularly grateful to Revd Ed Davis, Anglican and Co-ordinating Chaplain at Bristol, for extending the invitation to speak, and to Professor Gavin D'Costa for a stimulating conversation on my ideas over dinner afterwards. I did further work on the paper for a conference of Methodist interfaith practitioners later that same year at Cliff College, Derbyshire, and enjoyed the stimulating discussion it provoked. Chapter 4 arose out of a sabbatical research project I undertook in the Summer of 2014, some of which was written up for a chapter in *Contemporary Muslim–Christian Encounters: Developments, Diversity and Dialogues*, edited by Paul Hedges and published by Bloomsbury Academic in 2015. Chapter 4 is an expanded version of this earlier chapter, with an additional case study and further analysis. Throughout the book I reflect on experiences that were part of my ministry as a parish priest in Hyde Park, Leeds. Some of these experiences are written up in more detail in a book that was published by the Iona Community's publishing house Wild Goose Publications in 2009 under the title *A Heart Broken Open: Radical Faith in an Age of Fear*. I am grateful to Brill/Rodopi, Bloomsbury Academic and Wild Goose Publications for permission to use material here.

Notes

1 See for instance the report of the Commission on Religion and Belief in British Public Life, *Living with Difference: Community, Diversity and the Common Good*, available at www.woolf.cam.ac.uk/uploads/Living with Difference.pdf.

2 Alan Race, *Christians and Religious Pluralism: Patterns in the Christian Theology of Religions* (London: SCM Press, 1983).

3 Francis X. Clooney, *Comparative Theology: Deep Learning across Religious Borders* (Chichester: Wiley-Blackwell, 2010).

4 Mark S. Heim, *The Depth of Riches: A Trinitarian Theology of Religious Ends* (Grand Rapids, MI: Eerdmans, 2000).

5 Paul Hedges, *Controversies in Interreligious Dialogue and the Theology of Religions* (London: SCM Press, 2010) and Perry Schmidt-Leukel, *Transformation by Integration: How Inter-Faith Encounter Changes Christianity* (London: SCM Press, 2009).

6 See John Hick, *John Hick: An Autobiography* (Oxford: Oneworld, 2003), esp. chs 14, 15 and 16.

7 See Chris Allen, '"We Don't Do God": A Critical Retrospective of New Labour's Approaches to "Religion or Belief" and "Faith"', *Culture and Religion* 12:3 (2011), pp. 259–75.

8 Luke Bretherton, 'A Postsecular Politics? Inter-Faith Relations as a Civic Practice', *Journal of the American Academy of Religion* 79:2 (2011), pp. 346–77.

9 Shana Cohen, Sughra Ahmed and Alice Sandham, *Near Neighbours Report* (Cambridge: Woolf Institute, 2013).

10 See www.scripturalreasoning.org.

11 The PREVENT campaign has particularly come under activist scrutiny and criticism – see for instance the National Union of Students Black Students Campaign's analysis of the PREVENT Agenda at www.nus connect.org.uk/resources/preventing-prevent-handbook and *PREVENT: Why We Should Dissent: A Guide and Resource from Stand Up To Racism and Muslim Engagement and Development* (SUTR/MEND, 2017).

12 For excellent introductions to the methodology of practical theological reflection, see Heather Walton, *Writing Methods in Theological Reflection* (London: SCM Press, 2014) and Elaine Graham, Heather Walton and Frances Ward, *Theological Reflection: Methods* (London: SCM Press, 2005).

13 See Ray Gaston, *A Heart Broken Open: Radical Faith in an Age of Fear* (Glasgow: Wild Goose Publications, 2009).

14 See *The Stirrer*, 'EDL Racist Whipped up Hatred', 9 September 2009, an open letter to the West Midlands Police at http://thestirrer. thebirminghampress.com/edl-racists-whipping-up-hatred-09090901.html.

15 See Birmingham Spycams Summit Speech, 4 July 2010, at www. youtube.com/watch?v=ZleEWyc6pGs&feature=youtu.be.

PART I

Towards a Practical Theology
of Interfaith Engagement

I

Faith, Hope and Love

Pedagogy for Interfaith Engagement

Introduction

Exploring Theology of Religions

The threefold typology[1] proposed in Alan Race's *Christians and Religious Pluralism* has had many critics but has stood the test of time, as demonstrated at a recent conference held to reflect on its ongoing relevance.[2] Many still find it a helpful heuristic tool in approaching the engagement of Christians with other faith traditions. Race's three categories all have their contemporary proponents:[3] exclusivism, where there is no salvific efficacy in other faith traditions; inclusivism, where either other traditions can point one towards salvation in Christ or Christ works in those traditions to bring salvation; and pluralism, where all traditions that help people move from self-centredness to God or reality-centredness have genuine salvific efficacy. Although others have sought to expand the typology,[4] they remain committed to its value. However, the typology and theology of religions in general, with its focus on the salvific efficacy of the other, often descends into acrimonious theological contestation within intra-Christian exploration. I will argue that although the typology has had a long track record in academic theology of religions, it is not particularly well known within the Church. My experience of working with ordinands at an ecumenical theological college and among congregations is that the vast majority have never encountered the typology and are unaware of its

3

categories. However, many come to exploration of Christianity and interfaith engagement with real experience of engaging with people of other faith traditions. The typology is therefore, it will be argued, a useful pedagogical tool to enable reflection on attitudes to other faith traditions, and can be used to encourage intra-Christian theological engagement. I will seek to counter the claim that it necessarily has a pluralist bias, showing that although Race's original presentation had such a focus, others have used the typology to assert the positive nature of exclusivisms and inclusivisms alike. However, the critique of the typology – that it encourages the construction of fixed positions that drive an unhelpful theological contestation over the possibility of constructive theological dialogue – will be taken more seriously. Drawing on a brief comment by Michael Barnes in his *Theology and the Dialogue of Religions*,[5] I will outline how I have encouraged using the typology as a way for Christians to explore their practice in relation to other faith traditions and how this practice-orientated reflection encourages an affirmation of the value of each of the typology's categories and the necessity for intra-Christian dialogue. This chapter will therefore argue that using the typology alongside forms of reflective practice, rooted in real experiences of interreligious encounter, can enhance the confidence of Christians to engage constructively with the multifaith reality of our contexts, while also encouraging intra-Christian dialogue on religious plurality. This process enables people to express their own theological understandings in light of their practice and to reflect in turn on where they locate the primary source of accountability for that understanding.

Using the Typology in Theological Education

I normally begin any course of this kind by asking participants to reflect on a significant encounter with another faith tradition. Participants are encouraged to define 'significant' for themselves. The following are a small selection of responses gathered from ordinands and congregants in 2009.

Barbara, an 85-year-old woman, who attends a church in an area where 80 per cent of the population is Muslim, regularly talks about her faith and in turn learns about the faith of her Muslim taxi-drivers. She finds that they often ask her to pray for a personal or family need, as they take her to the weekly Bible study class she attends at her local Methodist church in inner-city Birmingham.

Siperire, a Methodist minister in Coventry, remembers when she worked for a nursing agency being assigned to a live-in post with an elderly Orthodox Jewish woman suffering from dementia, and having to learn about Kosher practices and finding herself entering into the rhythms of Jewish life.

Roy, who works for a small engineering firm in Solihull, developed a friendship over 12 years with a Muslim colleague, Ahmed. They often talked together about God, prayer and family life. Recently the firm made a number of people redundant. Ahmed lost his job and Roy kept his; this was a difficult experience for them both.

Roberta, a primary school teacher in Wolverhampton, tells a story of being challenged by Sikh children in her class because she had placed a Bible on the floor. One of the 10-year-old children in the class left her seat, came forward, picked up the book and placed it on her desk. This incident led to a class discussion on how different faith communities treat their 'holy books'. Roberta further reflected on the role of Scripture in Christian tradition and how it differs from that of other faiths.

Mandy, an NHS manager and an Anglican ordinand preparing for a curacy in Stafford, is a member of a reading group of 'professionals' that includes among its members three Hindus and three Christians. Recently, as part of a project for her training, Mandy asked the group if they would be willing to read the Old Testament book of Daniel. The generosity and interest with which her Hindu friends approached the book and the insights they gave caused Mandy to reflect on how open she would be to reading the Scriptures of other faith traditions.

A church from an evangelical tradition in a West Midlands town that has had a ministry to nightclubbers for some time – including serving tea, coffee and water – were approached by local Muslims during Ramadan, who wanted to join with them and offer food to revellers. The church agreed and a continuing relationship developed.

These encounters are by no means unusual, particularly for participants who live in the urban conurbations of the West Midlands, and sharing them in the class encourages an understanding that our theological reflecting is done in the reality of our lived experience. When we reflect on how we relate to the typology, such reflection is done with the stories of encounter with real people of other faith traditions present with us in the room.

From this initial exploration and sharing of stories of encounter I move on to present the typology to the class. The question, for me, then becomes *how* the typology should be presented. Race's original typology was an argument for a pluralist theology of religions and it is claimed to have an inherently pluralist bias built into its structure.[6] However, if one examines some popular presentations of the typology from more conservative theological approaches, it becomes clear that this is not necessarily the case. For instance, in her book *The Bible and Other Faiths: What Does the Lord Require of Us?* Ida Glaser, from a conservative evangelical perspective, presents the typology arguing that exclusivism is Christocentric, inclusivism is theocentric and pluralism is reality-centred.[7] The aim is clearly to present to her target audience the positive nature, for them, of the exclusivist position with its supposed unconditional affirmation of Christ. Meanwhile Veli-Matti Kärkkäinen, in an attempt to affirm mainline church inclusivism to a perhaps more conservative audience, chooses to present exclusivism as ecclesiocentric, inclusivism as Christocentric and pluralism as theocentric.[8] The bias in each of these presentations is towards exclusivisms and inclusivisms respectively. The typology can be presented therefore in a number of forms that privilege one of the types over another as the most appropriate, depending on the audience and their particular biases as well as those of the authors. My own presentational bias perhaps leans towards the inclusivist position, not necessarily because I hold to that myself but because I interpret that as being the position that might be defined as the one closest to official statements of both the Anglican and Methodist churches who sponsor most of Queen's students and who make up the membership of most of my classes in local churches. However, although the potential dangers for Christian integrity of the extreme ends of the continuum may be explored, I seek to emphasize that I believe all three positions can be argued for from within the Christian tradition. I also aim to present the typology in varied form, offering, first, a number of bullet points for each type and then, second, quotes from representatives of the type that also challenge easy dismissals of one type or another. Thus a quote from Barth is used, which reads as a strong exclusivist statement:

Religion is unbelief. It is a concern . . . indeed, we must say that it is the one great concern, of godless man . . . From the standpoint of revelation religion is clearly seen to be a human attempt to anticipate what God in His revelation wills to do and does do. It is the attempted replacement of the divine work by a human manufacture. The Divine reality offered and manifested to us in revelation is replaced by a concept of God arbitrarily and wilfully evolved by man.[9]

But then Barth's possible universalism is also mentioned, challenging the stereotype of exclusivism as condemning other traditions to hell.[10]

A quote from Rahner presents the anonymous Christian position:

Anonymous Christianity means that a person lives in the grace of God and attains salvation outside of explicitly constituted Christianity . . . Let us say, a Buddhist monk . . . who, because he follows his conscience, attains salvation and lives in the grace of God; of him I must say that he is an anonymous Christian; if not, I would have to presuppose that there is a genuine path to salvation that really attains that goal, but that simply has nothing to do with Jesus Christ. But I cannot do that. And so, if I hold if everyone depends upon Jesus Christ for salvation, and if at the same time I hold that many live in the world who have not expressly recognized Jesus Christ, then there remains in my opinion nothing else but to take up this postulate of an anonymous Christianity.[11]

However, then his later interview about mutual inclusivity is also raised,[12] challenging the accusation that inclusivism is inherently imperialistic in its co-option of other traditions.

Finally, I use a quote from Wilfred Cantwell Smith that argues for pluralism on strongly Christian grounds, challenging the assumption that pluralism leaves behind the Christian narrative in its presentation of itself.

> Those of us who have heard of these [other patterns of faith and religious tradition] and know something of them must affirm with joy and triumph, and a sense of Christian delight, that the fact that God saves through these forms of faith too corroborates our Christian vision of God as active in history, redemptive, reaching out to all people to love and to embrace them. If it had turned out God does not care about other men and women, or was stumped and had thought up no way to save them, then that would have proven our Christian understanding to be wrong.[13]

Once familiar with the typology, participants are asked to identify with one or other of the three positions. The emphasis here is not to commit oneself but to identify which affirms one's own position most closely, acknowledging that the reality may be more complex and considering the engagement with other faith traditions already reflected on at the start of the class. Participants are encouraged to place themselves on a continuum stretching along the room from conservative exclusivisms at one end to radical pluralisms at the other. The emphasis is on understanding the typology as a continuum rather than a set of fixed positions, on which people may move in different directions in their Christian journey of encounter with other faith traditions. When participants feel they have settled into a position they feel momentarily comfortable with, we take a look at the spread. At Queen's, which is theologically diverse, we usually have a spread of people across the continuum from 'moderate' exclusivisms to 'moderate' pluralisms and everything in between. Students are then encouraged to engage in conversation between the positions to offer to the whole group why they stand where they are, and to question others about their own stance. This often leads to robust defences and some questioning of exclusivist and pluralist positions especially. Students are also encouraged to reflect back to their own sharing of 'significant' encounters, to root their perspectives in the reality of experience of other faith traditions. They also reflect on how they wish to identify with aspects of the different types within the continuum; for example, some represent this physically by moving back and forth between inclusivisms and exclusivisms or straddling a perceived 'border' between inclusivisms and pluralisms. The physical representation of a position, the necessity to vocalize and dialogue with other Christians on this position and the need to relate it to the experience of engagement with those of other faith traditions allow the complexities of Christian interreligious engagement to arise. Finally, students are presented with an alternative way of reading the typology. Michael Barnes argues for a shift in interpreting the typology from a theology of religions to a theology of dialogue, seeing the classic positions as:

> theological *tendencies* which emphasise theological instincts or values – for example, the three theological virtues of faith, hope and love, which are to be developed within the actual process of dialogue – they can be understood not as mutually exclusive positions but as complementary perspectives which need somehow to be held together . . . 'Exclusivism' witnesses to that faith which speaks of what it knows through the specificity of tradition. 'Inclusivism' looks forward in hope to the fulfilment of all authentically religious truths and values. 'Pluralism' expresses that love which seeks always to affirm those values in the present.[14]

Typology as Tool for Reflective Practice

In the shift articulated above by Barnes, each of the types can be understood as representing one of the virtues of faith, hope and love (1 Corinthians 13.13), which are needed in order that effective dialogue take place with one another, whether between faiths or within the community of faith, but also as a self-reflective practice within the individual Christian. Each of these virtues needs expression in the discipleship of the Christian in their engagement with the religious other, in order for engagement to be true – a balancing of the three virtues in one's continued practice. Students are therefore encouraged to reflect on the dynamic of faith, hope and love in their past and future encounters and how the dynamic lives within them in their articulation of their theological perspective on interfaith encounter.

The approach outlined above disarms theological approaches that seek to do battle over how we should view other faith traditions. It helps us to recognize that each position brings something to the table of Christian interfaith engagement; a deep relationship with an essential virtue for the practice of creative discipleship and ministry in a multifaith world. In the context of theological training, where the classroom is often increasingly theologically diverse in its makeup, an ability to engender such intra-Christian dialogue is essential and also encourages a pedagogical approach drawing on Christian diversity, seeing diversity as a resource for enabling encounter with other faith traditions. The late evangelical theologian Clark Pinnock shows how such an approach works when he says of his own open evangelical proposal:

> one could say that my proposal is exclusivist in affirming a decisive redemption in Jesus Christ, although it does not deny the possible salvation of non-Christian people. Similarly, it could be called inclusivist in refusing to limit the grace of God to the confines of the church, although it hesitates to regard other religions as salvific vehicles in their own right. It might even be called pluralist insofar as it acknowledges God's gracious work in the lives of human beings everywhere and accepts real differences in what they believe, though not pluralist in the sense of eliminating the finality of Christ.[15]

The Praxis of Engagement – Learning through Conscious Encounter Seen as Spiritual Practice

A model of theological education for interfaith engagement that works with the tools of reflective practice, above, will emphasize the need for students to enter into an educative process in which they are encouraged into a conscious encounter with themselves, God and others in response to the multifaith contexts of today's world. This involves providing opportunities for engaging with different faiths, exploring what it means to be a Christian in a context that might be termed the growing 'multifaith consciousness' of our society, and experiencing dialogue as missional, theological and spiritual practice rooted in relationship with Christ. In this process three forms of engagement are emphasized and brought into dialogue for each student through experiencing interfaith encounter. An *engagement with other faiths* (interfaith dialogue), an *engagement with each other and the Christian tradition* (intra-Christian dialogue) and an *engagement with ourselves in relationship to God* (inner-self dialogue). This process draws on contemporary theories of theological reflection, such as the pastoral cycle, and narrative approaches to theology, such as Elaine Graham's 'theology of the heart',[16] which encourage reflexivity; but it also draws on older resources in the tradition for reflection, such as John Wesley's 'practical divinity',[17] and emphasizes the need to see our multifaith context as a God-given opportunity. Interfaith engagement can be seen as a spiritual practice, a means of grace that draws us closer to the God revealed in Jesus Christ.

The Content of the Engagements

As we have seen above, Barnes' critical analysis of the typology transforms it from argumentation on the salvific potential of the other into a dialogue on the virtues required for engagement, offering an alternative starting point for the Christian developing a deeper reflection on discipleship in a multifaith world.

This reflection on the faith, hope and love triad is augmented by a reflective process that asks in response to each encounter and experience on the course: 'What are the gifts, challenges and questions that I come away with from this experience?'

These experiences are also explored within the framework of reflection on the three 'engagements' of inner, intra and inter referred to above. Students are encouraged to reflect on how these three relate to each other in a self-reflective dialogue: do they prioritize one over the others? If so, why?

Students are recommended to maintain a reflective journal throughout the course, asking, 'Where is God in this dialogue?' This is essentially an application of the methods of practical theological reflection to the context of interfaith engagement.

The dynamic reflective model in Figure 1 is introduced in the classroom as a model to use, in engagement with other faiths, as opportunities are presented for 'crossing over'[18] to

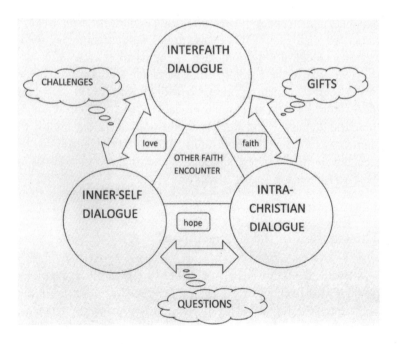

Figure 1: Dynamic reflective model.

other traditions in the course programme. Options, which are planned and timetabled into the course, might include among others: Qur'anic study groups; Sufi Dhkair; Langar at the gurdwara; Aarti at the mandir; Shabbat morning service at a synagogue; visiting a sangha and experiencing Buddhist meditation; Jummah prayers at a mosque. In such encounters individuals or small groups of students engage with people of different faiths in their own contexts through conversation and experiencing their community in practice. In addition to this, students are expected to engage in a disciplined fashion with the Scripture or practice of another tradition during the course through accessible translations and introductions. All this activity then is reflected on through the prism of the gifts, challenges and questions – faith, hope and love – and inner, intra and inter modes of reflection.

There is here then a change of emphasis from a theology of religions through Barnes' theology of dialogue to a theology of engagement that adopts a model of theological reflection rooted in contemporary understandings of practical theology. Barnes' faith, hope and love triad is opened up through an additional conversation with the inner, intra and inter triad and the reflection on the direct experience of the engagement in the gifts, challenges and questions mode of reflection; neither of the latter assumes or excludes the prioritizing of fidelity to traditional understandings of one's faith tradition. The emphasis is on the individuals' reflection on their own practice, where this practice leaves them in their relationship to God and which element – inner, intra or inter – they consciously prioritize to come to their understanding.

Dialogue vs Evangelism? Exploring Mission in Multifaith Contexts

As with theology of religions, contestation often features in explorations of missiology within Christian traditions, with proponents for evangelism and dialogue pitted at different ends of an argument. Although sophisticated missiological approaches to interfaith engagement exist, on the whole, easy categorizations and simplistic opposites of evangelism vs dialogue are the perceptions that are strongly represented in our churches and among ordinands at theological institutions. Moving away from a simplistic contestation of evangelism vs dialogue, a pedagogy with a practical theological focus shifts the emphasis from this false dichotomy towards reflection on the necessity of learning from each other in order to meet the challenge of our multifaith reality. One commentator has noted the necessity of occupying the risky ground between positions that overemphasize dialogue on the one hand or witness on the other.[19] The missional task is not to secure tradition or offer a safe, superficial relationship with our neighbours of other faiths but to take the risk, through encounter, that our understanding of our faith may change and that our relationships with our interfaith neighbours need to engage creatively with real difference. It is in this intra-Christian informed praxis of 'missional synthesis' that the tension between and the connection of dialogue and witness is lived creatively; it is a 'mission tension' in which growth occurs.

I draw on the work of Helen Reid to help ordinands at my theological college explore this mission tension and the need for different approaches to learn from and appreciate one another. While Director of Bradford Churches for Dialogue and Diversity (BCDD), Dr Reid sought to introduce students to different models of mission in her Bradford context, drawing on two case studies. I present the same case studies to students and ask them in small groups to explore the similarities between the two stories – 'What is it that is similar between the two projects?' This often poses a challenge to students in whom is engrained the understanding of binary opposites that these stories could be seen to represent. However, given the discipline of finding similarities, it has been surprising what is revealed – try it for yourself!

Two Stories from Bradford 2005

1 Presence ministry in Horton Grange, Bradford

Two Catholic Lay sisters lived – until very recently – in a shared house. Sr Mary explained her approach:

> My ministry stems from my commitment to serve Christ in his people as a member of the congregation of the Sisters of Mercy, founded to serve all people regardless of their culture or religion. How I personally engage in this is difficult to answer, it is nothing more than presence – walking daily the 'road less travelled' in respect, openness, friendship and understanding or the diverse peoples of this neighbourhood.

Sr Mary describes her neighbourhood as follows:

> There are at least eight nationalities and three if not more major faiths – Muslim, Hindu and Sikh. We all come from different backgrounds and perspectives and get on well on a general level although we do not engage in interfaith dialogue beyond generalities. Our diversity is a rich and as yet untapped possibility and it holds the key to a better future in which we will see the earth and all people as one sacred community. We discuss local issues at a local forum and people are becoming more aware of the need to take personal responsibility. At seven in the mornings, Roisin and I are in our street clearing litter and sorting things for recycling. It is small but a way of caring for each other and the earth. It has also engaged us in conversations about environmental issues that affect us all. We meet with others on the eleventh of every month at the Khidmat Centre [Community Centre run for Bradford Council for Mosques] for 'Interfaith Prayer for Peace'. Prayers are followed by a shared meal. Some people come for the prayers, some for the fellowship, some because they need a decent meal.

2 *The Jesus DVD project, Girlington, Bradford*

This area has the highest proportion of Pakistani Muslims in Bradford (over 80 per cent). This is an ecumenical project – Anglican, Methodist, Bradford Family Church, Baptist, URC and El Shaddai – although different churches get involved to different degrees. People from local churches distribute a letter to local houses, introducing themselves and saying they would like to call at this house. They then knock on doors, introduce themselves and offer to bring a copy of a DVD about the life of Jesus. If this is accepted, they call again and bring the DVD (whatever language is requested), asking if they might call again to ask for people's opinions about what they have seen. There is a positive local response in terms of quite a high level of acceptance of the DVD: double the average in an 'all white suburban area' – the kind of neighbourhood in which this project usually takes place. The church is pleased that it is an opportunity actually to offer a gift to people, and it seems that people are pleased to be offered a gift; one can imagine that in a culture in which giving and receiving is consciously acknowledged as the way to build relationships, this is not insignificant. At the doorstep there are sometimes requests for prayer and meaningful dialogue taking place. When Christians return again, it may be that no one has watched the DVD or it may be that a whole family has watched it. People can discuss it if they wish. Some individuals choose to become enquirers and there are particular groups, such as a Masala Group for this.

From a church perspective, people feel more connected with their local area. This year they have been surprised at the number of Eastern European people they have met – proof of what they had been reading in the papers. They feel encouraged by the many homes in which they are welcomed and happy to know more people when they walk in the streets.

Similarities

The similarities the students come up with usually look like this:
- to witness to Christ's love – it was often agreed that both projects sought to witness to the love of Christ;

- to be local – they were seen as locally rooted;
- long term – they had a long-term commitment to the area;
- everyday – related to people in their everyday lives;
- relational – they sought to develop real relationships;
- to take risks – they didn't remain in comfort zones but sought to take risks;
- prayer – prayer was at the heart of each project.

The question is then posed: 'What do these similarities tell us about the best of Christian missionary endeavour and our practice as Christians?' This often leads to reflections on the theology of the incarnation and its impact on the best missiology.

We then go on to explore what are termed 'distinctives'. The term is deliberate, seeking to move away from creating easy opposites and contestation towards a view of the 'differences' as potentially complementary rather than contradictory.

Distinctives

- Praying with people of other faiths – the sisters engaged in interfaith prayers *with* others.
- Praying for people of other faiths – the DVD project sought out prayer requests to pray *for* others.
- Emphasis on introducing people to Christ as Lord – a strong interpretation of Christ as Lord was present in the DVD project that was the thrust of how they wanted to introduce Christ to others.
- Emphasis on introducing people to Christ as servant – a strong interpretation of Jesus as servant was present in the activity of the sisters.

We then go on to consider how the two projects meet the Five Marks of Mission laid out by the Anglican Communion. These marks were established by the Anglican Consultative Council in the 1980s and 1990s precisely to challenge another contestation on mission in relation to evangelism and social justice. The ACC website introduces the Marks of Mission as:

1 to proclaim the Good News of the Kingdom;
2 to teach, baptise and nurture new believers;
3 to respond to human need by loving service;
4 to transform unjust structures of society, to challenge violence
   of every kind and pursue peace and reconciliation;
5 to strive to safeguard the integrity of creation, and sustain and
   renew the life of the earth.[20]

Mark 1 is normally understood as a summary statement that encapsulates the other four marks. When students analyse the DVD project and the sisters' ministry in light of the five marks, they often find that together, the two projects make a holistic representation of all the marks. Separated, each is lacking in significant marks of mission. We then consider what a dialogue on the Marks of Mission between the two Christian projects might do to each project's missionary endeavour – what they can learn from one another in order to enhance and develop a more holistic missional approach.[21]

The Reflective Model in Action – A Student's Reflections

The following is a submission from a student ordinand who was on the residential week-long intensive version of the course for ordinands at the Queen's Foundation in 2016. This piece is a written reflection submitted for assessment that requires students to use the modes of reflection outlined above. This reflection piece will be drawn from the journal that the student maintained throughout her exploration on the course and in post-course reflections. The student brings to the exploration her experience of working with Muslim refugees and also an interest in Islam. She comes from an evangelical Christian background and brings a concern to maintain a sense of theological integrity while wanting to engage fully. This mixture of experience and self-awareness leads to a rich exploration of her engagement with Islam through a visit to a mosque and engagement with the Qur'an and wider reading. She also reflects well on encounter with other students and the course material outlined above in both the exploration of theology of religions and missiology using the gifts, challenges and questions and inter, intra, inner modes of reflection to full effect. It is reproduced here with the student's full permission.

Simple Meetings Enable Transformation

3 April, after first session:
'I was concerned that Christ would be marginalized, thankfully the opposite seems to be true.'[22] This was my first gift. The challenge and question to my inner self was to be open to be changed during the rest of the week.

'Simple meetings enable transformation.'[23]

This reflective journal describes some of the gifts, challenges and questions I encountered within the faith of submission, Islam;[24] through the 'simple meetings' and dialogue facilitated within myself, my fellow Christians and with Islam, through the people I met at the mosque, the Qur'an and the module study material. I have chosen Islam because I am in contact with Muslim refugees on a daily basis and it was through the dialogue with Islam that I felt most impact. This reflection unfolds aspects of Islam's revelation to me about evangelism and my engagement with Muslim women.

4 April:
I stood at one end of the line as an exclusivist, unable to embrace Rahner's proposal of 'anonymous Christianity'. I struggled with the view expressed by some of my inclusivist and pluralist brothers and sisters in Christ that exclusivists demonstrate lack of love in evangelistic behaviours.

The discussion about our own position with regard to Race's typology of religion brought the predicted intra-Christian dialogue directly into the classroom. I felt challenged about how my genuine desire to honour 'the Great Commission' might be perceived by others. This deepened when we considered the five virtues of interreligious dialogue,[25] the greatest being love. I questioned myself, 'Were they right, possibly?'

The visit to the mosque turned this challenge into a gift. That evening my journal said: 'I felt defensive about being evangelized. On discussion with the rest of the group they felt the same.' This was an interesting moment for me as I reflected that 'others may have experienced those same feelings as a result of my enthusiastic evangelism previously'. I returned to the comments my peers had made earlier, responding with a new insight into how my behaviours may be perceived, and questioning 'How do I represent Christ's distinctiveness and "the Great Commission" through the virtues of interreligious dialogue?'

Our Muslim host described himself as 'a Muslim by choice', distinguishing himself from Muslims who are not faithful to the Five Pillars of Islam. Often those of other faiths assume Caucasian Europeans are Christian. I resolve 'to learn from my Muslim host and describe myself as a Christian by choice' when speaking to those of other faiths. During our visit, I became aware that while we share similar language often our meaning is very different. He repeatedly emphasized the Qur'anic view that God does not have a son. As guests, we did not feel comfortable to challenge this or apparent misquotations of the Bible, not only in relation to Jesus but also in relation to Adam and the Fall. He said that God forgave Adam. I wondered where that statement came from. We challenged ourselves: 'should be able to respond to this, but it seemed rude to do so at the time'. Later, I read the Qur'an and found a different narrative of the Fall. Adam is forgiven. I also found beautiful passages about God's forgiveness. I wrote: 'The Qur'anic text results in the absence of the doctrine of original sin, how would a Muslim understand Christ as saviour? How do I dialogue with my Muslim friends in the context of tahrif?' I felt that my language was ineffectual in dialogue with Islam.

The separation I felt sat in the women's area, undermined our host's assurance of Islam's appreciation of women, stating that it is men who are weak and distracted by women. 'This challenged my stereotypical view of inherent female oppression in Islam. Discussion confirmed this was shared by my peers.' The gift of transformation came through study. I understand that initially women were treated comparatively well in Islam. In general, Islam was viewed positively by Christians when it first emerged. Oppression of women arose through the influence of Judeo-Christianity following influence by Hellenistic traditions. Some suggest that the Patristic Fathers developed an inequitable view of women based on these views and the creation account in Genesis 2, which was incorporated into the Hadith narrative. The Qur'anic creation account does not feature Eve. The Qur'an describes spiritual gender equality. 'Did Christianity contribute to the oppression of women in Islam today?'

5 April:
Challenged again! When the quiet service of the sisters scored highest in effective mission as measured against all Five Marks of Mission and by the legacy of Constantinianism especially linked to evangelism, I reflected on my own practice and new understanding of Islamic history. 'Stanley Hauerwas' quote "make your life available to others in a way that they can help you discover ways you're implicated in violence you hadn't even noticed" provides the gift of a fresh lens to view mission'[26] and question: 'Can I be a guest rather than host?'

8 April:
'Muslim women aim to be like Maryam – that's new to me!' Friday's discussion about Islam's respectful understanding of Jesus and Mary gifted me a fresh sense of connection with Islam and a fresh language of hope and love. Mary is the only woman named in the Qur'an, named more than in the New Testament. As an evangelical, Mary has not had a prominent role in my faith compared with my Anglo-Catholic colleagues. The film about Mary highlighted key differences in the Qur'anic texts regarding the annunciation and birth of Jesus and in Jesus' identity. It invited me to explore my own Christian faith with my Muslim friends to gain a greater understanding of Mary. I can certainly learn from my Muslim friends if I am bold enough and humble enough to ask.

Panikkar stated: when you dialogue with somebody, look at your partner as a revelatory experience as you would – and

should – look at the lilies of the field.[27] I started the week concerned that Christ should not be marginalized. I have found
that in looking at other faiths, particularly Islam, I have seen
aspects of my own faith and witness in a new light. I felt no
need to reflect heavily on Christ's distinctiveness in my journal
because at no point did I feel it was under threat. I do feel
invited to join those of other faiths in their spirituality, confident in my own identity. So I have made plans to join a Muslim
colleague fasting for a couple of days during Ramadan.

In this reflection we see the student displaying a high level of
engagement with the course methodology and effective use of the
recommended modes of reflection in a natural and unforced way.
She also engaged well with theological questions and dug deeply
into Islamic tradition in order to understand her encounters and
to explore some of her reactions to experiences at the mosques
she visited. She showed an ability to describe her own process and
aligned this with thoughtful and engaging critical thinking and
questioning that wrestled impressively with a dynamic of openness
and maintenance of theological integrity. A high degree of reflexivity was shown and a real thirst for exploration and knowledge. The
student also resourced herself well in response to engaging questions on Islam, in particular, and displayed a significant engagement with the Qur'an, given the limited confines of the course.

The emphasis on the whole exploration of our understanding
of other faiths is to highlight the necessity for this kind of personal reflexivity and intra-Christian dialogue to enable a more
holistic engagement with other faiths that is faithful, hopeful and
loving and can enable a deeper relationship with our own faith.
The above reflection demonstrates this method well.

Conclusion

As I have said, engagement with other faiths in Christian theology
has traditionally been studied through the interpretative lenses
of theology of religions or missiology. In theology of religions

the question being addressed is the salvific status and efficacy of both the individual believer and their faith tradition: 'Who' is saved and 'How' are they saved? In missiology the approach has often been to learn about 'the other' in order to understand and approach them informed for apologetic and evangelistic encounter. In readjusting our interpretative lenses in a practical theological direction, we turn the focus away from 'analysing' the other, either in relation to their salvific efficacy or as targets for apologetic or evangelistic engagement, and instead focus on how encounter with other faith traditions has an impact on Christian self-understanding. The subject of exploration becomes ourselves and our relationship with others and with God. We move from a theology of religions whose subject is the other, to a theology of engagement whose subject is ourselves. This is not a narcissistic self-reflection but a spiritual practice rooted in the gospel: how do other faith traditions enable us to enter into a deeper relationship with Christ? And what challenges to our witness and self-understanding do they pose, which might be seen as enabling within us a truer witness to the love of God in Christ Jesus?

Notes

1 Alan Race, *Christians and Religious Pluralism: Patterns in the Christian Theology of Religions* (London: SCM Press, 1983).

2 See Elizabeth Harris, Paul Hedges and Shanthi Hettiarachchi (eds), *Twenty-First Century Theologies of Religions: Retrospection and Future Prospects* (Leiden: Brill-Rodopi, 2016).

3 Perry Schmidt-Leukel, 'Religious Pluralism in Thirteen Theses', *Modern Believing* 57:1 (2016), pp. 5–18.

4 See Paul F. Knitter, *Introducing Theologies of Religions* (Maryknoll, NY: Orbis, 2002).

5 Michael Barnes, *Theology and the Dialogue of Religions* (Cambridge: Cambridge University Press, 2002).

6 Barnes, *Theology and the Dialogue of Religions*, p. 8.

7 I. Glaser, *The Bible and Other Faiths: What Does the Lord Require of Us?* (Leicester: InterVarsity Press, 2005), pp. 28–33.

8 Veli-Matti Kärkkäinen, *An Introduction to the Theology of Religions: Biblical, Historical, and Contemporary Perspectives* (Downers Grove, IL: InterVarsity Press, 2003), pp. 165–73.

9 Karl Barth, 'The Revelation of God as the Abolition of Religion', *Church Dogmatics*, 1/2 (Edinburgh: T. & T. Clark, 1956), p. 301, cited in Knitter, *Introducing Theologies of Religions*, p. 25.

10 See Tom Greggs, *Barth, Origen, and Universal Salvation: Restoring Particularity* (Oxford: Oxford University Press, 2009).

11 Karl Rahner, *Karl Rahner in Dialogue: Conversations and Interviews 1965–1982* (New York: Crossroad, 1986), p. 135.

12 See Gavin D'Costa, *Theology and Religious Pluralism: The Challenge of Other Religions* (Oxford: Blackwell, 1986), pp. 89–91.

13 Wilfred Cantwell Smith, *Towards a World Theology: Faith and the Comparative History of Religion* (London: Macmillan, 1981), p. 171.

14 Barnes, *Theology and the Dialogue of Religions*, pp. 8, 184; emphasis in original.

15 See Clark H. Pinnock, *A Wideness in God's Mercy: The Finality of Jesus Christ in a World of Religions* (Grand Rapids, MI: Zondervan, 1992), p. 15.

16 See Elaine Graham, Heather Walton and Frances Ward, *Theological Reflection: Methods* (London: SCM Press, 2005), pp. 18–46.

17 For an example of using Wesley's understanding of the way of salvation and applying it to interfaith engagement, see Chapter 3 below.

18 See Ewert H. Cousins, *Christ in the 21st Century* (New York: Continuum, 1992), pp. 105–15.

19 Richard Sudworth, *Distinctly Welcoming: Christian Presence in a Multifaith Society* (Bletchley: Scripture Union, 2007).

20 See www.anglicancommunion.org/identity/marks-of-mission.aspx.

21 The necessity of such intra-Christian dialogue has been recognized in international explorations of mission in multifaith contexts in recent years – see for instance *Christian Witness in a Multi-Religious World: Recommendations for Conduct* (2011), published jointly by the World Council of Churches, the Pontifical Council for Interreligious Dialogue and the World Evangelical Alliance – www.worldevangelicals.org/pdf/1106Christian_Witness_in_a_Multi-Religious_World.pdf.

22 Ray Gaston, *A Heart Broken Open: Radical Faith in an Age of Fear* (Glasgow: Wild Goose Publications, 2009), p. 20.

23 Andrew Wingate, *Celebrating Difference, Staying Faithful: How to Live in a Multi-Faith World* (London: Darton, Longman & Todd, 2005).

24 Gaston, *A Heart Broken Open*, p. 93.

25 See Catherine Cornille, *The Im-Possibility of Interreligious Dialogue* (New York: Crossroad, 2008).

26 Stanley Hauerwas, from an interview with Colman McCarthy in *The Progressive*, April 2003.

27 Raimon Panikkar, *The Intrareligious Dialogue* (New York: Paulist Press, 1999), p. 1.

Beyond New Contestations

A Practical Theological Challenge
to Particularists and Pluralists

Introduction

In this chapter, building on the primary reflection on the typology and missiology in Chapter 1, which emphasized a dialogical and practical focus, I now examine more recent developments in the theology of religions that seek to replace the typology with a debate between pluralisms and particularisms.[1] I will seek to analyse this development using David Tracy's three disciplines of theology.[2] It will be argued that while pluralisms and particularisms represent explorations within theology of religions that are principally influenced by the fundamental and the systematic disciplines respectively, we require a greater concentration on developing what might be termed a theology of interfaith engagement, which is principally influenced by the practical discipline of theology – being built on a closer analysis of how Christians are actually engaging with their multifaith realities. I will also examine the appropriate concern of both recent particularist and pluralist writers to move beyond Eurocentric and modernist paradigms in theology of religions discourse, drawing on the work of the Argentinian philosopher of liberation Enrique Dussel and the Egyptian critical theorist Samir Amin. It will be argued that a practical turn in theology of religions can be helpfully informed by an engagement with Dussel's concept of transmodernity and Amin's reframing of 'global history'. The work of Raimon

Panikkar and Theo Sundermeier will then be explored to move us towards a practical theology of interfaith engagement that has a spirituality rooted in kenosis at its heart. Sundermeier's hermeneutical approach will then be applied to the experience of my own engagement with Islam over a number of years.

Particularism vs Pluralism?

As expressed at the beginning of the previous chapter, while many voices claim the end of the typology for theological understanding, my argument has been for its maintenance as a heuristic and pedagogical tool that, appropriately used, moves us beyond the old contestations of theology of religions (exclusivisms, inclusivisms, pluralisms), towards a dialogical, practical theology of interfaith engagement. In so doing I want to resist moves to reset the contestation boundaries as between pluralisms and particularisms. These perspectives seek to construct new contestations or 'isms' initially loosened by Barnes' theology of dialogue. However, perhaps as Barnes sought to read 'behind' the contestation of the threefold typology, we might read this new binary somewhat differently too.

In a thorough and extensive article, Richard Sudworth charts an Anglican theological engagement with Islam over 100 years.[3] From the missionary exclusivisms of the late nineteenth century to the dialogical explorations of the late twentieth century, Sudworth argues for what he terms an 'ecclesial-turn' in Anglican theology in its understanding of interfaith relations in the early part of the present twenty-first century. Drawing heavily on the document *Generous Love*,[4] Sudworth notes a change in approach:

> Where earlier Anglican documents suggested that the challenge of other faiths might provoke a new scheme of theologies of religions, an 'external discourse' shaping the Church's vision, Generous Love begins with God and the consequent nature of the Church within the life of God. What this turn reflects,

then, is not a new innovation in theology but a recovery of inherited traditions: a genuine ressourcement.[5]

Here Sudworth notes the influences of fashions in theology of religions on church exploration. His 'external discourse' refers to what he sees as the influence of the typology on previous church reports, most notably the Church of England's *Towards a Theology for Inter-Faith Dialogue*.[6] This has now been replaced by a theological exploration that, while open to engagement with other faith traditions, locates this engagement within a clearly Christian theological framework asserting the importance of the Trinity and the Church for understanding the reality of religious diversity. Here we see charted within Sudworth's exploration of Anglican engagement with Islam the supposed move from the typology to particularism. But it is not a move marked by heavy contestation with what has gone before; indeed it is only through Sudworth's meticulous analysis that the development is charted. In fact there is a strong affirmation in *Generous Love* of the value of theological plurality in interfaith encounter and of what has gone before: 'From every branch of Anglicanism, evangelical, catholic and liberal, missionary scholars, both women and men, contributed alongside local Christians in developing a theology for mission and dialogue through inter faith encounter.'[7]

Sudworth perhaps overstates the case of seeing in *Generous Love* a *conscious* shift from a pluralist influenced typology to a more particularist model. The affirmation of theological plurality does not point in that direction and the shift may be better understood as representing the changing nature of the Anglican Communion and the role of the Church of England within it. An increasing awareness of the international dimensions to dialogue has replaced a model of theological reflection that perhaps privileged local Church of England concerns and its identity as an established Church that addresses a wider audience than the committed Christian community.

Jenny Daggers has recently argued for a move towards particularism in engagement with religious plurality that seeks to locate this move firmly within a new contestation of theology of religions. For her, the combative approach is necessary to free inclusivist and exclusivist theologies from being defined by the pluralist bias she sees in the typology. In her book *Postcolonial Theology of Religions*, Daggers casts the net of particularisms widely, drawing into her analysis many theologians particularly from postcolonial contexts that might previously have been claimed by pluralists.[8] Into this net she also draws a particularist understanding of theologies of dialogue and comparative and feminist theologies alongside the postcolonial theologies of religion from Asia that allow her to argue for a Eurocentric bias in the typology.

In an earlier book, Paul Hedges also argues for a new division between what he terms pluralisms and particularisms as the new contestation in theology of religions. A little less combative than Daggers, and arguing from a pluralist perspective that claims to learn from and dialogue with particularisms, Hedges charts much of the same territory as Daggers, including postcolonial critiques of Eurocentric understandings of religion, comparative and feminist theologies to argue for a theology of 'radical openness' and 'mutual fulfilment' that maintains 'Christian integrity'. Although his is essentially a more dialogical argument than that of Daggers, Hedges does stray into the area of strong contestation, arguing at one point for reading exclusivisms as fundamentally 'unchristian', and forcefully against the orthodoxy presented by particularist perspectives.[9]

It is into these new contestations that David Tracy's categorization of the disciplines of theology might provide a helpful interpretative tool. In his book *The Analogical Imagination*, Tracy outlines three disciplines in theology: the fundamental, the systematic and the practical. He summarizes their particular bias of interest as follows:

> Fundamental theologies will be concerned principally to provide arguments that all reasonable persons, whether 'religiously involved' or not, can recognize as reasonable . . . Systematic theologies will ordinarily show less concern with such obviously public modes of argument. They will have as their major concern the re-presentation . . . of what is assumed to be the ever-present disclosive and transformative power of the

particular religious tradition to which the theologian belongs. Practical theologies will ordinarily show less explicit concern with all theories and arguments. They will assume praxis as the proper criterion for the meaning and truth of theology.[10]

Using Tracy's categories of disciplines, I would want to argue that the pluralist versus particularist argument is between theologies whose emphasis is on the fundamental and systematic respectively. This can be seen in the changes noted by Sudworth, which I would maintain provide a better reference for understanding the shifts in emphasis noticed in *Generous Love*. Daggers recruits to her particularist camp many theologians who seek to engage with religious diversity through the use of Christian language and categories alone, or where dialogue with the other leads to what she says is a Christianity *recentred* rather than what she perceives as Christianity *transcended* in pluralist theologies and within the thrust of the typology – even when it is presented in a systematic form as in Alan Race's original book (see Chapter 1). However, some of those she sees as successfully recentring rather than transcending Christianity are indeed people who have previously been identified with the pluralist theology of religions. How can this be so?

One might argue that the Christianity-transcended element within many presentations of the typology and in pluralist theologies of religions points to a stronger influence in such theologies of the fundamental, with its concern to articulate beyond the Christian community.[11] The concern of those engaged in recentring, on the other hand, is to develop a systematics that gives intra-Christian reasons for engaging in dialogue while also preserving and reasserting Christian language and symbols as adequately interpretative of religious plurality, which arguably can be done by anyone, from exclusivist to pluralist.

Hedges concentrates on a panoramic exploration of theology of religions and religious studies and, while seeking to articulate in parts a specific Christian narrative for interfaith engagement, does so within a framework that might be argued to fit Tracy's fundamental category. For him the exploration of comparative theology moves us not to a recentred systematics but to the possibility of a new fundamental horizon – interreligious theology.[12]

It might be argued that, free of the polemics of contestation, neither Daggers nor Hedges is cavalier in their use of the similar theological and wider resources they recruit to develop their arguments, but represent different emphases in their approaches that are systematic and fundamental respectively.

It might also be argued that the options of transcending tradition or recentring on tradition are not alternatives but a process that is indeed necessary for Christian theology in a multifaith context. We might look back at the dynamic we identified in missiology between secure tradition and secure relationship as being the places of safety and non-engagement with the dynamics of encounter. In theological terms, such extremes might be represented by some theologians from particularist and pluralist camps – Paul Griffiths, for example, in relation to particularism and John Hick in relation to pluralism. Griffiths' radical refusal to see any possibility of cross-communication between traditions ensures that encounter with the other will have no impact on Christian theological reflection:

A religion ceases to be a religion . . . when one or more of the elements essential to it is lost by abandonment or transformation; and one religion is different from another just when it is not possible for the same person to inhabit a Buddhist form of life that loss of any contact with members of the Sangha, the monastic order, is also loss of something essential to their religion, and as a result amounts to abandonment of it. Or, it may seem to a Muslim who adds belief in the Trinity to his Islamic form of life that he has replaced it thereby with a new one because the theism that informed the old religion has been transformed. By contrast, it may seem to a reform Jew who becomes Orthodox that she has not abandoned or replaced her earlier religious form of life, but only modified it as one might modify one's marriage by adding to it a severer and more demanding observance of the disciplines of love. And finally, it seems reasonable to say that Greek orthodox Christianity and Gulag Tibetan Buddhism are different religions in much the same way that it's performatively impossible to belong to both at once – to be a sumo wrestler and a balance-beam gymnast, or natively to live in the house of English and the house of Japanese.[13]

Hick's deconstruction of Christian uniqueness – and any other traditions' uniqueness – elides the potential of engaging creatively with real differences and facing the discomfort of encounter with others who perceive the world in ways radically different from our own, particularly when he claims all traditions can be judged and understood through the interpretative lens of pluralist set criteria.

> I propose that we apply to religious experience within the other great world faiths the same principle that we apply to our own, namely critical trust: it is to be trusted except when we have reason to distrust it. And the test by which both Christians and people of the other faiths judge the authenticity of religious experience is its moral and spiritual fruit in human life . . . a transformation of human existence from natural self-centredness to a new orientation centred on the Transcendent, the Ultimate, the Real.[14]

Daggers perhaps strays into 'securing tradition' territory when she recruits, too easily, postcolonial 'pluralists' for 'particularism'. In fact the relevant point she makes, that the distinctive nature of Stanley Samartha's and Aloysius Pieris' Asian theologies are lost in an appropriation into a Eurocentric pluralism, can also be made in her recruitment of them to a postmodern Eurocentric particularist project which is part of the ongoing largely Western-dominated debate on theology of religions. Daggers is too ready to redefine such creative engagements with religious plurality from postcolonial contexts under her redefined particularism in a manner that is dangerously close to appropriation and undermines the very particularity and creatively context-driven motivations of their understandings by co-opting them under a reasserted Christian systematic orthodoxy, which largely remains defined by resources from the unacknowledged context-driven Euro-American theological traditions. And Hedges strays close to 'securing relationship' territory when he seeks to cut off any form of exclusivism as a legitimate form of Christian self-understanding.

Instead of such potentially intellectually violent contestation as that outlined above, a recognition of the difference of approach between 'fundamental' and 'systematic' might allow for a greater dialogue between these positions, might undermine the attempt to construct hardened 'isms' that battle for the loyalty of other theologies – comparative theology for example – and might raise questions as to the truth and appropriateness of such fixed articulations, clearly providing resources for the exploration of both. As with the faith, hope and love triad outlined by Barnes, we are not saying here that these theologies are *only* fundamental or systematic; we are arguing that they *emphasize* one element over the other. Similarly, using Tracy's disciplines, we might notice the significant absence of theologies *emphasizing* the practical discipline among those engaging with our multifaith reality.

Towards a Practical Theology of Interfaith Engagement

A practical theological emphasis brings fresh understandings into the dialogical process that is theological exploration of religious diversity, which require a different starting point from those employed by a theologian influenced by the more systematic or fundamental modes of reflection. The practical theologian would give primacy not to communication with wider disciplines in the Western academy, or to a strong fidelity to the symbols and language of the Christian tradition, but to an engagement with and examination of the diverse nature in contemporary cultures of the practice of religiosity and spirituality both within but also beyond the confines of official adherence to a faith tradition, bringing that lived human experience into dialogue with the tradition and other reflective disciplines, allowing the findings to shape and inform Christian praxis in our contemporary contexts. A practical theology of interfaith engagement is different from comparative theology that seeks to analyse the texts and spiritual or liturgical practices of a tradition, to bring them into dialogue with the texts and liturgical or spiritual practices of Christian tradition. A practical theology of interfaith engagement would be concerned with gathering quantitative and qualitative data on *actual* Christian experience in our multifaith world and how particular Christians experience the encounter with other faiths, enabling these voices to be more fully represented in theological discussion of interfaith engagement by drawing on the methods of theological reflection developed in contemporary practical theology – the pedagogy developed in Chapter 1 is one such approach.

Both Daggers and Hedges, coming from their systematic and fundamental methodological emphases, are concerned to free their reflections from a form of Eurocentric modernism and engage with postcolonial and postmodern critiques of theology of religions. Similarly, any practically focused theology of interfaith engagement would be required to do the same and would need to focus on how interfaith engagement might drive Christian praxis towards liberative practices for human flourishing in a violent and radically unequal world; it is to that concern we now turn.

Challenging Eurocentrism

Enrique Dussel, an Argentinian philosopher, has been developing an understanding of modernity that strongly challenges its universalizing claims and brings it into dialogue with more traditional non-Western epistemologies to enhance the project of human liberation. A Christian who has influenced and been influenced by liberation theology, Dussel has sought to outline what he calls 'transmodernity' – an attempt to transcend modernity's limitations through a critique of its development and a more open attitude to traditional epistemologies. This, Dussel maintains, is a critique of modernity that unlike the postmodern critique, which is an argument from within, comes from beyond its Eurocentric confines. Postmodernism can, potentially, replace the dismissal of tradition as 'backward' in modern discourse, with a false openness to the other and difference that is located in a disintegrating relativism. As the Muslim scholar Ziauddin Sardar has commented:

> Postmodernism is what comes after modernity; it is 'post' in terms of time; it is a natural culmination of modernity. This is why it is sometimes described as 'the logic of late capitalism'. It represents a linear trajectory that starts with colonialism, continues with modernity and ends with post-modernity, or postmodernism.[15]

Postmodernism, while affirming difference and diversity and critiquing potential totalizing tendencies in modernist epistemologies, is still located within a Eurocentric framework and is essentially therefore a critique from within Western epistemology, which Sardar sees as still potentially limiting and oppressive. Sardar also argues that in its radical forms, postmodernism, like modernity, seeks to undermine traditional epistemologies: while modernism sought to locate traditional forms of knowledge as 'backward', postmodernism undermines traditional understandings through its radical relativizing of all knowledge and a surface embracing of difference that hides the continued marginalization of non-Western cultures and societies 'by suddenly discovering otherness everywhere':

> The postmodern prominence of the Other becomes a classic irony. Instead of finally doing justice to the marginalized and demeaned, it vaunts the category to prove how unimportant, and ultimately meaningless, is any real identity it could contain.[16]

Dussel locates the beginning of modernity at the end of the fifteenth century and the so-called 'discovery' of the Americas by Christopher Columbus in 1492,[17] when the Portuguese and Spanish invasions set up an alternative power base to the then rising economically dominant Chinese dynasty. This, he maintains, sees the beginning of a shift of the location of global power from the Islamic world to the European, what he calls 'first modernity'. Europe then becomes increasingly seen as the centre of the 'world-system', with the rest of the world on the periphery. This development is confirmed and fully established only by the eighteenth century, when Dussel sees the period of second modernity come into being. European power is legitimized and upheld by a 'myth of modernity'; at its foundation is the 'the myth of emancipative reason', where humanity frees itself from immaturity to express itself through the gift of reason to the highest degree. This is epitomized, Dussel maintains, in the work of Immanuel Kant in the late eighteenth century. According to Dussel, the whole concept of 'modern civilization' is founded on this idea. He also sees the work of Hegel as a development of these earlier Kantian notions, into a theory of world history that writes Europe into the centre of a historical process in which the history of Asia is a pre-history to European development, with dominance running from the ancient Greek world through the Roman Empire into the medieval Christian world and on to modern Europe. Dussel writes: 'I am trying to emphasize that the unilineal diachrony Greece-Rome-Europe is an ideological construct that can be traced back to late-eighteenth-century German romanticism.'[18] This Eurocentric understanding of the historical process marginalizes whole cultures and civilizations and does not accept the reality of European marginalization in the fifteenth century: 'Latin Europe of the fifteenth century, besieged by the Muslim world, amounted to nothing more than a peripheral, secondary geographical area situated in the westernmost limit of the Euro-Afro-Asian continent.'[19]

The fascinating complexities of history and the development and flow of ideas between cultures[20] is ignored or erased in such a history and, dangerously, a narcissism of the rule of subjectivity – the subject of the modern Western man – determines the measurement of the humanity of 'others'. A failure on the part of non-European others to appreciate the superiority of a Western understanding of the world leads modern Western man to violence to assert the supposed emancipatory power of Western thought in whatever form that takes. Dussel writes: 'Modernity as myth always authorizes its violence as civilizing whether it propagates Christianity in the sixteenth century or democracy and the free market in the twentieth.'[21] There is a complete failure to comprehend the 'other' and a complete dismissal of their culture. Dussel acknowledges and draws on the work of writers such as Emmanuel Levinas, who show categorically that the Western concept of pure subjectivity is violent and dangerous in its refusal to acknowledge dependencies on the other. But as Smith has pointed out, Dussel goes further, questioning Levinas' ability really to creatively engage with 'otherness':

> It is Dussel's contribution to say that all these formulations still circulate within a philosophical system that is closed in on itself. The other that must be faced within this system still in a sense has a face that is only recognizable to the spectator insofar as it serves as an example of something that can be taken into account within pre-existing registers.[22]

It might be argued, therefore, that if we apply Dussel's approach to the theology of religions and particularly the salvific typology, we can see that it raises questions as to its potential captivity to an oppressive Eurocentric modernity.[23] The exclusivist paradigm in its various forms is either a version of the conquistadors' confrontation with the other, which leads to their damnation, or the Hegelian denial of the right of any system to exist that is not the one perceived to be blessed with 'Universal Spirit'. The inclusivist paradigm, in the style of Levinas and the other partial critiques of modern subjectivity, wants to acknowledge the other but only with the pre-existent registers of their own theological system. The pluralist paradigm combines aspects of both the exclusivists, when it insists on the developmental superiority of pluralism, and the inclusivists, when subsuming under the auspices of Western philosophical categories (after Hick) the religions, spiritual practices and philosophical categories of the marginalized traditions of the world. Alternatively, the particularist perspective draws on postmodernist resources that affirm a form of what the Egyptian scholar Sadir Amin calls 'culturalism', which potentially denies, through a relativized 'traditionalism', the possibility of collective universal projects for human flourishing. Amin, who is credited with coining the term 'Eurocentrism', comes from a North African and Islamic context, a Marxist economist and commentator who has been central in critiquing a view of history that asserts European hegemony and ignores, particularly from his point of view, the role of the Islamic empires in global history. Like Dussel, he seeks not a total dismissal of the Enlightenment but a liberating engagement with it from the 'periphery', and hence is quite critical of postcolonial approaches that developed out of the work of Edward Said. A critic of economic developmental progressivism of both the Euro-American right and left, although a radical secularist, as a creative Marxist he does not dismiss the potential of religious traditions in contributing to future visions of human transformation, affirming Christian liberation theology while strongly critiquing 'political Islam' but also attacking Western Islamophobia.

Dussel's and Amin's concern is to bring other voices beyond the Eurocentric into focus and to enter into real dialogue with modernity in order to help transform it, not reject it – hence transmodernity. There is a need, therefore, in relation to the theology of religions, to free the typology and particularism from the confines of modernity and postmodernity, often represented in the more strident advocates of pluralisms and particularisms respectively, and instead move us towards a possible transmodern theology of interfaith engagement, enabling a more truly dialogical approach that lives with a rational modern consciousness of the reality of the plurality of religions but draws from the wells of its tradition to approach the 'other' with openness and allows those others to help form our theology. One possible example of the latter would be to base a Christian theology of religious pluralism on a dialogue with Qur'anic understandings of religious pluralism that emphasize the God-given nature of religious pluralism and diversity.[24]

A Christian transmodern theology of religion includes allowing other faith traditions, speaking from beyond the Eurocentric dominating discourse, to help Western Christianity free itself from the sometimes reductionist epistemological confines of modernity and postmodernity that have a hold on both conservative and liberal theologies. The captivity of the Church to Eurocentrism is perhaps demonstrated in what Kenneth Cracknell has identified as the partial reading of the Scriptures present in the dominating hermeneutical key of the *Heilsgeschichte* or 'salvation history' perspective that still dominates liturgical lectionaries and ecumenical missionary understanding to this day. One of the key

proponents of this interpretation was Oscar Cullman, who interpreted the biblical story as a redemptive history. Cracknell says:

> The shape of this history is like an hour glass: large at the top then
> narrowing down to a very small aperture then widening out again.
> The story of the redemptive community begins with Abraham
> and all the people of Israel. It includes the events of Passover and
> Exodus and the covenant of Sinai . . . but then begins the 'pro-
> gressive reduction' (until) it becomes limited to one person: the
> one faithful Israelite, Jesus of Nazareth. But after Easter Day the
> story of redemption changes completely. It becomes even wider.
> From the tiny company of apostles, it expands to the ingather-
> ing of the day of Pentecost. Then the movement from Judea and
> Samaria out into Asia Minor and on into Europe. In the eigh-
> teenth and nineteenth centuries the birth of worldwide missions
> took the gospel message to the ends of the world.[25]

Cracknell identifies serious problems with this analysis and draws
on Asian Christian experience of religious plurality to critique
it. However, we can also read Cullman and salvation-history
perspectives through the lens of Amin's and Dussel's critique of
Eurocentrism and identify this reading's total captivity to the
'myth of Europe' as the centre of history after the ancient world.
In this perspective the stories of ancient Christian traditions in
North Africa, Iraq, India and China are ignored and Cullman's
understanding is totally in line with understandings that argued
for the 'civilizing' mission of the Church in European expansion
in modernity and a Christianity captivated by and contributing to
an understanding of the world that affirms imperial and capitalist domination. A practical theology of interfaith engagement will
seek to contribute to breaking this connection through a praxis
that finds resources within the tradition for radical transforma-
tive engagement with traditions beyond the Eurocentric, and is
critical of imperial and capitalist systems – which one liberation
theologian has called 'The Ideological Weapons of Death'[26] – over
the God of life who drives praxis in the direction of an ethic of
resurrection.

Raimon Panikkar – A Transmodern Theology of Religion?

The late Raimon Panikkar, often labelled a 'pluralist', didn't always sit easily with this designation and presents a very different understanding of religious diversity from the Western philosophically influenced 'common ground or core'[27] pluralism articulated by John Hick, which until lately tended to dominate debates on the pluralist perspective. What is also interesting about Panikkar is that he often worked from non-Western Enlightenment philosophical foundations and epistemology in his pluralist theology, creating a synthesis between Christian, Humanist, Hindu and Buddhist ontological understandings in his 'cosmotheandric' principle.[28] In his rejection of the dominance of post-Enlightenment epistemology as well as in his concentration on developing a way of being in relation to the religious other, Panikkar might be said to exhibit transmodern impulses in his work.

Panikkar's explorations have for many years prioritized a theology and hermeneutics of the experience of dialogue and pluralism over the articulation of an overarching rational explanation of religious diversity. In *The Myth of Christian Uniqueness*, the collection that launched the pluralist paradigm on to the theological scene, Panikkar's essay sat uneasily alongside some of the others.[29] In his response to that essay, in the volume critical of the pluralist call to 'cross the Rubicon', Rowan Williams stated: 'Panikkar goes a long way to establishing his claim that he offers something other than either classical "inclusivism" or conventional liberal pluralism, and I believe that he . . . provides guidelines for an authentic theology of interreligious engagement.'[30]

Panikkar's essay[31] is concerned to appropriate the typology in a manner not dissimilar in process from that articulated by Barnes in the previous chapter. Panikkar sees the typology not as antagonistic, fixed theological positions but as attitudes related to the forming of Christian identity that exert different influences in different contexts through a dynamic interplay of geography, history and personal experience. Geographical context has certainly played a major role in the unfolding evolution of

Christian identity since, as biblical tradition has it, those early Judean Jewish 'people of the way' became identified by Gentile others as 'Christians' in Antioch, who themselves increasingly embraced and formed this new religious movement that became the Church. Geography is joined, of course, with history, as the Jewish radical sect that preached the arrival of a peculiarly unexpected Messiah became a Gentile religion that propagated pacifism and a countercultural way of life, but whose missionary success in the Roman-dominated world led to its eventual accommodation into a religion of the Empire; a process that might be seen as beginning with the conversion of Constantine but the seeds of which were perhaps sown some time earlier.

This geographical–historical dynamic is fruitfully explored by Panikkar as he outlines a river-based metaphorical typology of the evolution of Christian self-consciousness that takes us on a journey from the witnessing charismatic and exclusive faith of the Jordan and the Jewish beginnings, to the institutional, creedal-believing orthodoxy of the imperial Tiber, on to a postcolonial open spirituality that is represented by the Ganges and the engagement with multireligiosity and the wider world. This reframing of the typology frees it from its captivity to a reductionist Eurocentric modernism. These are not just, or even primarily, historical and geographical realities of Christian history but an existential typology of the personal journey and the resource wells for the contemporary Christian whose identity will be formed by an ongoing dialogue with this geographical–historical dynamic as she develops a religious attitude in her increasingly multireligious world, which is in dialogue not only with those 'religious others' but internally with the radical sectarian exclusivist Christianity of the Jordan, the institutional and imperial inclusivist Christendom of the Tiber and the personal spirituality of pluralistic Christian-ness represented by the Ganges.

Panikkar's creative reworking of the modern classic salvific paradigm of Christian theology of religions, with its exclusivist, inclusivist and pluralist camps, focuses on the spirituality of the transmodern Christian pilgrim in her approach to religious pluralism, privileging an articulation of the subjective religious

experience of dialogue – a hermeneutics of religious experience – over supposed objective theological construction about the
salvific efficacy of other traditions and meta theories of theologies
of religion. Panikkar is concerned to affirm a search for a genuine Christian-ness, a Christic attitude, as he calls it, for a pluralist
context that is not so much about a theological contention about
salvation as much as a Christian engagement with the reality of
religious pluralism and the opportunities this holds for a deeper
Christian practice and understanding, a practice that Panikkar
professes elsewhere in his writings took him on a journey in which,
he says, 'I left [Europe] as a Christian; found myself a Hindu; and
I return as a Buddhist, without having ceased to be a Christian.'[32]
Here he perhaps exhibits a transmodern consciousness in relation
to religion that Dussel says:

> achieves with modernity what it could not achieve by itself – a
> co-realization of solidarity, which is analectic, analogic, syn-
> cretic, hybrid, and mestizo, and which bonds centre to periph-
> ery, woman to man, race to race, ethnic group to ethnic group,
> class to class, humanity to earth, and occidental to Third
> World cultures. This bonding occurs not via negation, but via
> a subsumption from the viewpoint of alterity.[33]

As Roberto Goizueta has said, 'the notion of transmodernity refers
not so much to a new way of thinking as to a new way of living
in relation to Others'.[34] Central to this is the concept of analec-
tics, which prioritizes the voice of the excluded other from dominating 'totalities'. These voices help to undermine the oppressive
elements of the totality of – in this case Eurocentric – modernism
and help to reframe it as a potentially liberative project. We
could argue that such an approach might be an appropriate one
for particularly Euro-American Christians in their approach to
other faith traditions. In an analectical relationship, such traditions may enable an undermining of Christianity's captivity to
the oppressive totality of Eurocentrism and free it to speak again
with a voice of hope and salvation, a process also underway in
the theologies of Samartha and Pieris, from postcolonial contexts,
mentioned above.

Kenosis – A Transmodern Christian Way of Living in Relation to Religious Others

It is in the process of encounter, as Panikkar has shown, that a theology of engagement with the reality of religious plurality in our current context should be concerned. Similarly, Martha Frederiks has also pointed out that this is perhaps best articulated as a form of interreligious hermeneutics, usually associated with the interpretation of texts;[35] hermeneutics has also been explored as a discipline in communication theory. This has led to an interreligious hermeneutics that acts as a way of interpreting the encounter with 'the religious other', exploring what happens in the process of interreligious encounter and how understanding this can enable us to adopt appropriate theological responses from our tradition to our multireligious context. Frederiks points to Theo Sundermeier as someone who has done considerable work in this area. In an essay, 'Aspects of Interreligious Hermeneutics',[36] Sundermeier categorizes a process of four levels of engagement with other religious traditions: on the first level the other religion is experienced as alien and even threateningly different. This step requires distance as the tradition is perceived and observed. The second level is that of participatory observation, as Sundermeier says, as one becomes more caught up with the signs of the tradition and a certain level of sympathy will enter the consciousness as one goes deeper into an engagement with the other tradition through its symbols – its rites, its teaching, the ways it creates community – and through this one enters the third level of engagement, which, according to Sundermeier, is only possible if one gets involved in the other faith tradition and 'exposes one's self to its fascination – at least for a moment. This is no longer a matter of participatory observation but of "compassionate experience".'[37]

At this level one experiences the religious practices of the other tradition and encounters the sacred texts of the tradition. Increasingly one finds oneself making comparisons with one's own tradition and communication becomes possible; here on this third level, as much as is possible, the religion should be seen as it is experienced by its practitioners. This leads to the fourth level, where the deepening encounter leads to what Sundermeier describes as the other tradition becoming a 'temptation'. At this level our own religious self-understanding is called into question and challenged: 'Now the other religion becomes a call, an inquiry to my own faith, an appeal to decide where I belong.'[38]

Such vulnerability, Sundermeier accepts, is not what is necessarily called for by our dialogue partners. However it is, he maintains, what is called for by the Christian call to love. It is this call that makes the Christian religion, he argues, so contested. Sundermeier locates this vulnerability in Christianity's kenotic structure, the call to self-emptying love at the heart of the gospel: 'It must abandon itself and has to get deeply involved with the other religion.'[39]

This is perhaps why, he reflects, the missionary movement became so much a focus for the push towards a serious engagement with other religious traditions in both mainline Catholic and ecumenical Protestant movements: the mission to convert the world often tied into imperialisms' expansionist projects became the experience of individual missionaries being converted themselves, to a deeper engagement with the reality of God through encounter with other faith traditions, in what might be seen as an analectic process rooted in a kenotic theological praxis. It might also provide a way of understanding some contemporary engagements with other faith traditions in our current context, particularly in relation to Islam and its 'otherness' and marginalization in the culture of 'the clash of civilizations'.

Interreligious Hermeneutics and My Engagement with Islam

When I first came across Sundermeier's analysis I was excited by how it spoke to my own experience of engagement with Islam. Back in the early 1990s, at the awakening of my interest in interfaith encounter, I was particularly drawn to the meditative practices of Buddhism and the radical plurality of Hindu traditions. I increasingly became aware of Islam on the geo-political stage in the 1990s and questioned the increasing presentation of Islam as a 'dangerous other' in relation to 'the West' and early presentations of Islamophobia in political discourse, but my own personal distancing from engaging with Islam in interfaith encounter also rested on prejudices of what I saw as an overly text-based literalistic tradition, and I avoided courses on Islam in my undergraduate degree. During my Master's degree at Lincoln Theological College I had the privilege of studying under Hugh Goddard at Nottingham University and took a course on Christian–Muslim relations, but this was still motivated more by a wish to understand the dynamics of 'Islam and the West' rather than an interest in Islam for Islam's sake. Through this period I was displaying a growing engagement with Sundermeier's first level of interreligious hermeneutics, with the sense of difference and threat moving to increasing levels of observation and growing perception. It was a few years later, when I became a vicar in an area with a significant Muslim population and three mosques in my parish, that I was moved into Sundermeier's second and third levels of participatory observation and 'compassionate experience'.

Coming into the parish of St Margaret's and All Hallows in 1999, I quickly became aware of the presence of Muslims in the area and felt compelled to make friends and visit mosques. One of the things that struck me early on was this communal experience of Ramadan – how gently visible the practice is; and although I was not directly involved I found myself moved by and appreciative of the prayers and the fasting going on around me. Within a couple of years I felt moved to participate. At first I began on my own, quietly fasting for just one day in solidarity with my Muslim neighbours, then the following year for a week, then the year after that for the whole month. Then the next year again I fasted for the month, and also read an English translation of the Qur'an in order to try to understand the way of Islam more deeply.

My earlier equivocation on Islam was dissipated by an increasing engagement with Muslims and interest in the traditions of Islam for their own sake; a developing 'compassionate experiencing' of the tradition was especially notable in my experience of Ramadan, as I wrote at the time in my journal:

> It's not easy to let Ramadan pass you by if you live and work in close proximity to Muslims. It is not that Muslims go about showing off their fasting during the holy month; it's more that you notice a different pace of life, a different tempo. It is a month for reflection on God and a conscious compassion and carefulness in your dealings with others; for a deepening of spiritual practice. As one Muslim scholar says: This month is a feast . . . not of noise, but silence; not of banquets but restraint; not of forgetfulness but remembrance. This month is a feast for the faith.

I increasingly participated, as the comments above testify, but it was in the second year of joining the fast, in which I also read the Qur'an, that I began to move towards what Sundermeier sees as the other tradition becoming a 'temptation'. It is here that his statement quoted above, 'Now the other religion becomes a call, an inquiry to my own faith, an appeal to decide where I belong', became a reality. During Ramadan 2005 I kept a diary in which I increasingly reflected on my engagement with Islam and the questions and openings it raised for how I understood my own tradition and my increasing sympathy for its own self-understanding. In contrast to my earlier resistance to Islam's textual rootedness, on day two I reflected:

> Christian Islamic scholar Wilfred Cantwell Smith says the Qur'an for Muslims is 'the eternal breaking through time; the knowable disclosed; the transcendent entering history and remaining here, available to mortals to handle and to appropriate; the divine become apparent'. The way Smith talks of the Qur'an echoes how Christians sometimes talk of the Incarnation. Is it any wonder that Muslims treat the book with such reverence, placing it on the highest shelf, keeping it well covered and handling it with care? How different to our battered and tattered bibles, with underlining and scribbles in the margins: the sites of wonderful contestation and argument

of interpretation. How close to the Catholic treatment of the elements, in the understanding of the real presence of Christ at the Eucharist; touching, holding Divinity in the palm of our hands in the form of Book or Bread. How different, too, though: the confusion of the broken body on the cross and the disorientation of resurrection, compared with the commanding guidance and assured authority of the spoken word of the Qur'an.

It was also during this Ramadan that my years of participatory observation and increasingly compassionate experience in mosques during Jummah prayers, sitting at the back reciting the Lord's Prayer internally or increasingly silent in my heart and allowing the prayers of others to fill my soul, seemed inadequate as what I came to call the 'wave of surrender' became an increasing 'temptation'. In Sundermeier's terms, by day 20 of the fast I wrote:

> Went to Grand Mosque iftar on Saturday night. I forget how young and multicultural the GM is. Met a lovely convert called Yousef and a Tunisian guy called Assad. Had some really nice conversations. I am going to return tonight and also go to the recitation, as Assad says it's the best he knows in Leeds. Again I felt drawn to join in the wave of surrender, but didn't. I would really love to be able to do this. In fact I would love to regularly attend mosque and participate in this as part of my own spiritual discipline. Need to think and pray about this more and look into working out what I am doing, a theology, a sense of keeping and developing spiritual and theological integrity . . . But do like the idea of exploring the question: what am I doing by joining in the wave of surrender? Can Christians join in Muslim prayers with integrity? What do different Muslims say about this?

By the following day I had entered into the experience and taken on the temptation, but a temptation rooted in a sense of calling based in my Christian faith echoing Sundermeier's call to love as the motivation for my 'temptation'.

I joined in at both Maghrib and Isha and Taraweh and every-one was very happy for me to do so. Hassan was there also and very friendly and welcoming. There is something special about the Grand Mosque in how international it seems and also quite informal. Children run around the mosque after prayers, playing just like at the Ahlul Bayt, and there is the power of praying with hundreds of others joining in the wave of surren-der, although I still feel a little too self-conscious. After what I said yesterday it seemed silly not to join in. The recitation last night was really beautiful and the Taraweh finished with some very powerful intercessory-type prayers, almost char-ismatic, people crying the prayers were very lamentational – powerful stuff. I am still forming answers to the questions I posed myself yesterday: something about crossing boundaries, something about openness, something about the call of Christ to dare to risk disapproval, something powerful too about lov-ing the unloved. Everyone, including myself in part, is afraid, cautious, suspicious of Muslims; it's deep in our psyche; it's part of what we inherit; it's rooted in the 'sins of our fathers', so to speak. I want to give the message to Muslims that their tradition is one in which I find beauty and depth, challenge and sustenance, and I want to open my heart more fully to God who is known in the mosque and I want to know God more profoundly by allowing Muslims, and particularly Islam, to work in my heart so that my vision of God expands and becomes fuller, truer. God wants me to receive and so I am opening my heart to Islam; yes, as I said last week, I long to share, but I also at this stage just want to open my heart and allow God to give me what he feels I need to guide me on this journey and I feel Jesus/Isa is with me. Would Jesus have stayed out of a house of prayer? How can I enter into mosques where hundreds are praying to the God of Abraham and not join in? How wonderful to sit on the floor after prayers and eat and talk about faith with fellow believers. There is the importance of the integrity of my faith tradition but more important surely is acknowledging the integrity of God. If I believe in and love God, must I not also seek him in the mosque and through Islam and indeed through those who have embraced Islam?!

After that Ramadan I often joined the line at Jummah prayers at the Grand Mosque during my time at All Hallows. After I left and moved to a new context, the necessity and the pull to participate dissipated and I have never since done so. This has led me to reflect on the experience as one that included elements that were related to the particularity of my context and the relationships established at the time and connected to the experience mentioned above of a process of transcending and recentring. However, the transcending did not involve a 'leaving behind' of my tradition or even a sense of 'crossing over' but was rooted in a spiritual practice coming out of a sense of a Christic call to deeper engagement at the time in Islamic prayer.

Reading the Bible as an Anti-Imperial Text – Undermining Accommodation to Capitalism and Empire

Part of the analectic openness we are exploring is the need to recover in that process the radical anti-imperialism of Jesus and the early Church. The 'one and only Saviour' language of the New Testament, which is so often used to dismiss the challenge of other faith traditions, is, many have recently argued, better interpreted as a resistance to empire.[40] The early Church grew up in the shadow of the Roman Empire with its claims to power and the claims of emperors to be divine: the language of the New Testament in its supposed exclusivism is addressing the context of idolatrous worship of the false gods of empire and wealth. The early Christians developed countercultural communities that challenged the Roman and Greek worlds' structured and fixed hierarchies.[41] The earliest creed, 'Jesus is Lord', was in direct rebellion to the claims of the divinity of the emperor. The radical gospel that Paul proclaimed was in direct contrast to and excluded the hierarchies of the Greek and Roman political and familial structures. These exclusive claims of the gospel are relevant to us today, when we are seduced by the pull of counterallegiances, be that to government, a political party, to the ideologies of nationalism

and patriotism, capitalism and militarism. The great religions of
the world are allies in this struggle, most importantly when they
help us in their critique to identify this accommodation. Another
excerpt from the Ramadan diary explores this dynamic:

> Today again I came across passages that are interesting in rela-
> tion to the Qur'anic understanding of the other People of the
> Book and their revelations:
>
> And there are, certainly,
> Among the People of the Book,
> Those who believe in Allah,
> **In the revelation to you**
> **And in the revelation to them.**
> Bowing in humility to Allah:
> They will not sell
> The signs of Allah
> For a miserable gain!
> For them is a reward
> With their Lord,
> And Allah is swift in account.
> (3:199; my emphases)

This is the sense I've got from my reading so far: that this
idea of Islam as a way of being is universal, a point of contact between People of the Book and Muslims. There are those
who practise Islam and those who don't. The historical context of some of the surahs concerning Jews and Christians
does appear to put Muhammad in a traditional Old Testament
prophetic role: challenging the Ahl al-Kitab (the People of the
Book), as the OT prophets challenged the people of Israel,
to return to the original calling and move from unjust practices that do not show them as truly submitting to God's will.
Esack[42] points out that the descriptions in the Qur'an that say
Jews and Christians have distorted their Scriptures could easily
be referring specifically to the context of the Muslim communities' direct experience of particular Jews and Christians and
their roles in politics and exploitation of the poor, and their

claims to be superior to others simply because they were Jews or Christians. The distortion that the Qur'an talks about in the communication of the Torah and gospel could be read as a deliberate misinterpretation and abuse of Scripture in order to exploit and oppress, not as a comment that the Scriptures themselves are inherently distorted.

Is this a basis for contemporary dialogue? The need for the Abrahamic faiths to act as prophetic correctives upon each other. How might this understanding help us to challenge misinterpretations of Christianity that promote the 'War on Terror' and Islamophobia? How might we present to Muslim friends and dialogue partners the challenge of Jesus's way of the cross that is not an imperialist attempt to convert others to Christianity but a gift to enable Islam?

Too often, equation is made between the religions of the Greco-Roman world in the New Testament and the religions we are aware of in our midst today. But the comparison could be argued to be false. A closer correlation to the religions of the Greco-Roman world with their worship of war and commerce would be the idolatrous commitment to a religion of militarism and consumer capitalism, as certain liberation theologians have demonstrated.[43] In the Roman-dominated ancient world, complex systems of worship in cultic and civic religions were aligned to worship of the Roman emperor to appease and curry favour with the primary imperial controllers of the ancient world.[44] Without such an analysis, we can easily fall into traps that dismiss other religions as idolatrous while partaking in the idolatrous worship of the system of global capital ourselves. As an example, during a residential course for theological students on interfaith engagement, a visit to a Hindu mandir was one of the options for the students to encounter as a small group. The hospitality they received was experienced by the majority of the students on the visit as gracious and generous. Included in this was a meal of vegetarian curry and rice. A small number of students declined the offer of food, despite the fact that the visit coincided with lunch. On dialogue with other students it was discovered that those who declined had done so for fear of accepting food offered to idols. The irony of this and the dangers of such an approach were demonstrated when the students chose to eat instead at a local McDonald's on the way back to college as an alternative to the hospitality and generosity of the local Hindu community, prompting other students to ask them if they weren't committing idolatry by doing that instead.

Beyond Particularism vs Pluralism towards a Liberation Theology of Interfaith Engagement

What Panikkar and Sundermeier represent is what we might call, after Dussel, a transmodern concern, more with the practice of dialogue and encounter as the basis for theological reflection than with the construction of grand salvific theories, and an equally transmodern concern to truly understand the 'other' on their own terms and learn from their world view in an attitude of solidarity and mutual enquiry that recognizes the need to move beyond the dominating Eurocentric confines of modern and postmodern thought while embracing the best of these traditions, but relativizing Eurocentrism through a serious consideration of non-modern Western epistemologies. Theology of religions becomes, in the process, a liberation theology committed to encountering truth in the epistemologies of the religious other, marginalized either by an imperialist form of Christian exclusivism or by the ideology of secularism and the philosophy of instrumental reason, while also standing against the idolatrous worship of the market and militarism.

Classical pluralists may want to challenge the former concern when they perhaps see it as a postponing of the inevitable need to 'cross the Rubicon'. However, Sundermeier's intimation about the centrality of the kenotic impulse at the heart of Christianity is an enticing one in relation to this possible criticism, for it provides a way the Christian tradition itself, at its heart, has the resources for approaching our contemporary context with an affirmation of a Christocentric theology that encourages a deep and vulnerable encounter with the other, while subverting our captivity to epistemologies of Enlightenment rationalism and postmodern relativism into what might be termed a transmodern theological epistemology. This is based in a spiritual practice rooted in a biblical exploration of the meaning of Christ's self-emptying path alongside a modern consciousness of the reality of religious plurality, while having a true respect for the epistemology of the other and learning from it.

Classical pluralism's insistence on the questioning of biblical and traditional Christological formulations is often based on too limited a reading of the Christian tradition and the history of the Church. Hick's sometimes dismissive attitude to his own Christian tradition and the possibilities for construction of a constructive theology of religions from within exposes an overreliability and false security on epistemologies of the Enlightenment and modernity and postmodernity's reductionist approach to religious knowledge.

As Barnes says about John Hick's critique of the history of Christian theology:

> That there is truth in what remains a sketchy outline is clear; Christianity has at times been both proudly exclusive and naively inclusive of the other. But that is not the whole story, and Hick's sometimes sweeping generalizations inevitably ignore elements of an important counter-tradition.[45]

A kenotic practical theology of interfaith engagement might be a possible contribution to this countertradition: a theology that encourages the Christian disciple to enter into the process outlined by Sundermeier and engage with other faith traditions, through 'compassionate experience' and 'vulnerability'. It also poses a challenge to those postmodern-influenced postliberals and 'particularists' who argue that the priority is Christian self-description in the context of good neighbourliness,[46] for in such a kenotic theological practice, Christian self-description is in the practice that impels one into a deeper engagement and interest in the other through the call to love. This isn't a call to a condescending love based on superiority but a love that comes out of a radical humility and openness rooted in an understanding of the revelation of God in Christ. This alternative path seeks to liberate the Church from the confines of a modernity defined by imperialism and capitalism as kenosis participates in an analectic process of transmodernity, transcending the excesses of pluralism's and particularism's accommodation to modernity and postmodernity and recentring on an understanding of the call of Christ through engagement with other faith traditions from the periphery of Eurocentrism's domination.

Notes

1 See Jenny Daggers, *Postcolonial Theology of Religions: Particularity and Pluralism in World Christianity* (London: Routledge, 2013) and Paul Hedges, *Controversies in Interreligious Dialogue and the Theology of Religions* (London: SCM Press, 2010).

2 David Tracy, *The Analogical Imagination* (London: SCM Press, 1981), pp. 47–98.

3 Richard Sudworth, 'Anglicanism and Islam: The Ecclesial-Turn in Interfaith Relations', *Living Stones Yearbook 2012* (London: Melisende, 2012), pp. 65–105.

4 Anglican Communion Network for Inter Faith Concerns, *Generous Love: The Truth of the Gospel and the Call to Dialogue* (London: Anglican Consultative Council, 2008).

5 Sudworth, 'Anglicanism and Islam', p. 91.

6 Anglican Consultative Council, *Towards a Theology for Inter-Faith Dialogue* (London: Church House Publishing, 1986).

7 Anglican Communion Network for Inter Faith Concerns, *Generous Love*, p. 7.

8 Daggers, *Postcolonial Theology of Religions*. Daggers presents a very sympathetic reading of both Aloysius Pieris and Stanley Samartha, both of whom contributed to the volume that launched the pluralist position on to the international theological stage (John Hick and Paul F. Knitter (eds), *The Myth of Christian Uniqueness: Toward a Pluralistic Theology of Religions* (Maryknoll, NY: Orbis, 1987)).

9 Hedges, *Controversies in Interreligious Dialogue*.

10 Tracy, *Analogical Imagination*, p. 57.

11 This is an argument made by Chester Gillis in his defence of Hick's pluralist hypothesis, which he argues should be read and critiqued as philosophy of religion rather than theology – Chester Gillis, 'John Hick: Theologian or Philosopher of Religion?', in Sharada Sugirtharajah (ed.), *Religious Pluralism and the Modern World: An Ongoing Engagement with John Hick* (Basingstoke: Palgrave Macmillan, 2012), pp. 137–51. I would include Hick's hypothesis as a form of Tracy's fundamental theology in its

apologetic nature as an argument for the rationality of religious belief –
John Hick, *An Interpretation of Religion: Human Responses to the
Transcendent*, 2nd edn (Basingstoke: Palgrave Macmillan, 2004).

12 Hedges, *Controversies in Interreligious Dialogue*, pp. 252–3.

13 Paul Griffiths, *Problems of Religious Diversity* (Oxford: Blackwell,
2001), pp. 10–11.

14 Hick, *Interpretation of Religion*, p. xxvi.

15 Ziauddin Sardar, 'Beyond Difference: Cultural Relations in the New
Century', in Ehsan Masood (ed.), *How Do You Know? Reading Ziauddin
Sardar on Islam, Science and Cultural Relations* (London: Pluto Press,
2006), p. 295.

16 Ziauddin Sardar, *Postmodernism and the Other: The New Imperialism
of Western Culture* (London: Pluto Press, 1998), p. 13.

17 It is interesting to note that the first World Parliament of Religions
in 1893 was held as part of the 'World's Columbian Exposition', the celebration of the 400th year since Columbus' 'discovery (sic) of the New
World'. This might be seen as the first event of the Interfaith movement
that is linked to the Christian Pluralist hypothesis. As Diane Eck says
in her introduction to the published papers of the parliament, 'on the
whole . . . the predominant vision of the parliament was . . . the dawn-
ing of a new era of unity and universalism'. There is something telling
about the link of the parliament to Columbus and locating the pluralist
hypothesis in the family of what Dussel calls 'second modernity'. See
Richard Hughes Seager (ed.), *The Dawn of Religious Pluralism: Voices
from the World's Parliament of Religions, 1893* (La Salle, IL: Open
Court, 1993). Daggers also picks up on this connection in her work.

18 Enrique Dussel, 'Europe, Modernity, and Eurocentrism', *Nepantla:
Views from the South* 1:3 (2000), p. 465.

19 Dussel, 'Europe, Modernity, and Eurocentrism', p. 468.

20 For instance, the fascinating flow of Greek philosophy between
Christian and Islamic cultures.

21 Enrique Dussel, *The Invention of the Americas: Eclipse of the 'Other'
and the Myth of Modernity* (New York: Continuum, 1995), p. 71.

22 David Geoffrey Smith, 'On Defrauding the Public Sphere, the Futility
of Empire and the Future of Knowledge after "America"', *Policy Futures
in Education* 1:3 (2003), p. 495.

23 Kenneth Surin, 'A "Politics of Speech": Religious Pluralism in the
Age of the McDonald's Hamburger', in Gavin D'Costa (ed.), *Christian
Uniqueness Reconsidered: The Myth of a Pluralistic Theology of Religions*
(Maryknoll, NY: Orbis, 1990), pp. 192–212.

24 For Qur'anic understandings of pluralism, see Asma Afsaruddin,
'Celebrating Pluralism and Dialogue: Qur'anic Perspectives', *Journal of
Ecumenical Studies* 42:3 (Summer 2007), p. i; Reza Shah-Kazemi, *The

Other in the Light of the One: The Universality of the Qur'ān and Interfaith Dialogue (Cambridge: Islamic Texts Society, 2006); Pim Valkenberg, *Sharing Lights On the Way to God: Muslim–Christian Dialogue in the Context of Abrahamic Partnership* (Amsterdam: Rodopi, 2006), pp. 150–62. See also how I pick up on this in Chapter 5 below.

25 Kenneth Cracknell, *In Good and Generous Faith* (Werrington: Epworth, 2005).

26 Franz J. Hinkelammert, *The Ideological Weapons of Death: A Theological Critique of Capitalism* (New York: Orbis, 1992).

27 Douglas Pratt, 'Pluralism, Post-Modernism and Inter-Religious Dialogue', *Sophia* 46:3 (2007), pp. 243–59.

28 See Raimon Panikkar, *The Cosmotheandric Experience: Emerging Religious Consciousness* (New York: Orbis, 1993).

29 Raimon Panikkar, 'The Jordan, the Tiber, and the Ganges: Three Kairological Moments of Christic Self-Consciousness', in Hick and Knitter (eds), *Myth of Christian Uniqueness*, pp. 89–116.

30 Rowan Williams, 'Trinity and Pluralism', in D'Costa (ed.), *Christian Uniqueness Reconsidered*, p. 12.

31 Panikkar's essay was expanded and published later in a collection of his works: *A Dwelling Place for Wisdom* (Louisville, KY: Westminster/John Knox Press, 1993), pp. 109–59. It is from this source that my comments are taken.

32 Raimon Panikkar, *The Intra-religious Dialogue*, rev. edn (New York: Paulist Press, 1999).

33 Dussel, *Invention of the Americas*, p. 138.

34 Roberto S. Goizueta, 'Locating the Absolutely Absolute Other: Toward a Transmodern Christianity', in Linda Martín Alcoff and Eduardo Mendietta (eds), *Thinking from the Underside of History: Enrique Dussel's Philosophy of Liberation* (Lanham, MD: Rowman & Littlefield, 2000), p. 189.

35 Martha Frederiks, 'Hermeneutics from an Inter-Religious Perspective?', *Exchange* 34:2 (2005), pp. 102–10.

36 Theo Sundermeier, 'Aspects of Interreligious Hermeneutics', in Martha Frederiks, Meindert Dijkstra and Anton Houtepen (eds), *Towards an Intercultural Theology: Essays in Honour of Jan A. B. Jongeneel* (Zoetermeer: Meinema, 2003), pp. 67–75.

37 Sundermeier, 'Aspects of Interreligious Hermeneutics', p. 73.

38 Sundermeier, 'Aspects of Interreligious Hermeneutics', p. 74.

39 Sundermeier, 'Aspects of Interreligious Hermeneutics', p. 75.

40 See for instance the work of Richard Horsley and Joerg Rieger.

41 See E. Elizabeth Johnson, 'Apocalyptic Family Values', *Interpretation* 56:1 (2001), pp. 34–44.

42 Farid Esack, *The Qur'an – A User's Guide* (Oxford: One World, 2005), ch. 2.

43 Hinkelammert, *Ideological Weapons of Death* and Ulrich Duchrow and Franz J. Hinkelammert, *Property for People, Not for Profit: Alternatives to the Global Tyranny of Capital* (London: Zed, 2004).

44 See for instance Richard A. Horsley, *The Liberation of Christmas: The Infancy Narratives in Social Context* (New York: Crossroad, 1989) and Joerg Rieger, *Christ and Empire: From Paul to Postcolonial Times* (Philadelphia, PA: Fortress Press, 2007).

45 Michael Barnes, *Theology and the Dialogue of Religions* (Cambridge: Cambridge University Press, 2002), p. 9.

46 This is the description Paul F. Knitter gives to the attitude to dialogue of postliberal theologians like George Lindbeck, William Placher and Paul Griffiths – see his *Introducing Theologies of Religions* (Maryknoll, NY: Orbis, 2002), pp. 183ff.

3

Interfaith Engagement, Non-Violence and the Way of Salvation

Interreligious friends are becoming interreligious activists. Perhaps better, the shared need to act is becoming the occasion to form and deepen friendships. This has been exemplified in recent meetings of the Parliament of World Religions. There, countless men and women from religious communities seek to respond to the challenges facing the earth and all its inhabitants. They sense that their religious response, if it is to be meaningful and effective, must be interreligious. No matter how different they are, religions must 'get their act together' in order to act together.[1]

Both art and Christianity require skills hard won, but the skills to be a Christian are finally matters of life and death.

The Christian practice of nonviolence is one of these sets of skills required by the Christian conviction that the powers that draw on our fear of death have been defeated . . . What the church has to give to the world is a politics of nonviolence made possible by a people who have learned through worship to speak truthfully to one another . . . We can only begin to understand the violence that grips our lives by being embedded in more determinative practices of peace – practices as common and as extraordinary as prayer and the singing of hymns.[2]

In many ways these two quotes exemplify opposing positions in the exploration of faith involvement in political activism. On the one hand the first, from Paul F. Knitter, who is a well-known Christian pluralist, argues for an interreligious contribution to tackling the issues of our time. This interreligious contribution is exemplified for Knitter in examples that he cites in his *One Earth, Many Religions*.[3] For Knitter, the common cause is that of the 'suffering other', and in focusing on this, interreligious activists avoid the endless debates about religious difference and concentrate their interreligious activities on engaging in actions to enhance a sense of 'global responsibility'. On the other hand, Stanley Hauerwas, as one of the 'new traditionalists', as defined by the American pragmatist Jeffrey Stout,[4] and someone from whom the new particularists in theology of religions would also draw, argues for a Christian engagement rooted in the particular practices of Christian non-violence. There is little room in Hauerwas' scheme for the kind of interfaith dialogue and action envisioned and enacted by Knitter – Hauerwas would clearly balk at what others[5] have perceived as the Kantian emphasis in Knitter's ethics, which limits the particularity of Christian discipleship to a purely motivational drive, fulfilled in a more universalist interreligious perspective. For Hauerwas, it is important to assert the truth of the particular practices of Christian non-violence rooted in the experience of the ministry, death and resurrection of Jesus Christ – this is the only way Christians can truthfully engage in the world. To dilute Christian discipleship into an interreligious ethic for the common good would be to surrender faith to pragmatism and to forgo the necessary eschatological witness of the Church.

When it comes to interfaith encounter, Hauerwas directs us to his mentor[6] John Howard Yoder[7] and a little-known essay that Yoder wrote in 1976[8] while in Jerusalem, to intimate at an approach to interfaith dialogue and action rooted in Yoder's commitment to a politics and ecclesiology firmly located in Christological non-violence, undermining the dominance of models of what he refers to as 'Constantinianism'. Yoder had an innovative reading of Christian history. He followed the radical reformation in arguing that while the early Church lived a Christological pacifism, the fourth-century Church compromised with Constantine and went to war.[9] The Church adopted Constantinianism. Constantinianism, for Yoder, is an arrangement whereby the Church's attitude towards violence and money shifts away from the New Testament pattern of pacifism and suspicion of wealth, towards a 'responsible' ethic suitable for running a society of people who do not confess Jesus as Lord. It was this Constantinianism that led among other things to the Crusades and church compliance with colonialism. Interestingly, in his work, Yoder also located signs of unfaithfulness in the early pacifist Church, which began to shun the Jewish roots of its faith in favour of respectability in the Gentile world.[10] Yoder argued for the necessity of the 'disavowal of Constantine' as a central tenet of a form of Christian interfaith engagement that drew on the Christological pacifism of the radical reformation tradition from which he came. Yoder's call to repentance for the years of imperialist Constantinian Christianity, as a first step in interfaith dialogue for the Western Christian, is a different type of critique of triumphalism and its implications for Christological understandings than is present in the pluralist critique outlined clearly by Knitter in his Christological sequel to his *One Earth, Many Religions*,[11] where, stripped of the false claims to supremacy of the theologies of orthodox Christianity, Christ becomes the unique motivational drive for Christians to enter alongside others, with different unique motivational drives, a universalist liberationist practice that goes beyond the particularity of each tradition. This type of approach has been well critiqued by many who see in it the same oppressive tendencies present in traditional Constantinianism, this time in the guise of the philosophies of post-Enlightenment modernity and the totalitarian universalisms of globalization.[12] Alternatively, for Yoder, recalling the truth of Christ's call to non-violence and servanthood, and its very centrality for Christian praxis, should elicit from Christians a move to the Christian practices of repentance and conversion in the face of the other, not in the form of the meeting of religious establishments in conferences and official dialogues and statements, but in the everyday relationships in local and particular contexts with those of other faiths; not in order to practise a universalist liberationist ethic, but to practise a deeper faith in Jesus Christ as Lord through defenceless witness to Christ's peace.

Community repentance is called for in the New Testament epistles. Yet somehow since Constantine it was decided that the church must be indefectible. It might change the whole tone of interfaith encounter if instead of saying, 'we still think we are right, but you may be right, too,' or, 'Yes, that is a wrong idea but that is not what we really meant,' Christians were to receive the grace to say, 'We were wrong. The picture you have been given of Jesus by the Empire, by the Crusades, by struggles over the holy sites, and by wars in the name of the "Christian West" is not only something to forget but something to forgive. We are not merely outgrowing it, as if it had been acceptable at the time: we disavow it and repent of it. It was wrong even when it seemed to us to be going well. We want our repentance to be not mere remorse but a new mind issuing in a new way – metanoia.'[13]

The Walk of Reconciliation as 'Disavowal of Constantine' – A Case Study in Repentance

Nine hundred years ago, our forefathers carried the name of Jesus Christ in battle across the Middle East. Fuelled by fear, greed and hatred, they betrayed the name of Christ by conducting themselves in a manner contrary to His wishes and character.

The Crusaders lifted the banner of the Cross above your people. By this act, they corrupted its true meaning of reconciliation, forgiveness and selfless love.

On the anniversary of the First Crusade, we also carry the name of Christ. We wish to retrace the footsteps of the Crusaders in apology for their deeds and in demonstration of the true meaning of the Cross. We deeply regret the atrocities committed in the name of Christ by our predecessors. We renounce greed, hatred and fear, and condemn all violence done in the name of Jesus Christ. Where they were motivated by hatred and prejudice, we offer love and brotherhood. Jesus the Messiah came to give life.

Forgive us for allowing His name to be associated with death. Please accept again the true meaning of the Messiah's words: 'The Spirit of the Lord is upon me, because He has anointed me to bring good news to the poor. He has sent me to proclaim release to the captives and recovery of sight to the blind, to let the oppressed go free, to proclaim the year of the Lord's favour.' As we go, we bless you in the name of the Lord Jesus Christ.[14]

So said the statement of the Walk of Reconciliation, an evangelical charismatic initiative that had its roots in the March For Jesus movement of the 1980s and 1990s. I originally came across this initiative when Lynn Green was invited by the Together for Peace group in Leeds, to address the worshippers at the Grand Mosque, located in the parish where I ministered in Leeds. Having read this statement, Lynn then spoke of the motivation of the Walk of Reconciliation. He was listened to by a couple of hundred worshippers who had stayed behind following Jummah prayers on a Friday afternoon to hear this talk. People were clearly moved and surprised; the Grand Mosque had an international congregation, many with links in the Middle East. The story of the Reconciliation Walk is a fascinating one in which leading evangelical missionaries, some of whom had been pivotal in the March For Jesus movement, decided to 'walk' the path of the First Crusade on the 900th anniversary of its beginning in 1096 and apologize for the Crusades. In an interview three years later towards the end of the walk, Lynn Green reflected on the impact of the walk on his own understandings of mission and Islam:

Personally, it's challenged some of my theology and especially my missiology. But I'm convinced that God gives grace to the humble and is opposed to the proud. I have noticed that for Muslims, Jews, and Orthodox Christians (these are our three audiences, as it were), that as we go to them in humility, saying we deeply regret what has been done in the name of Jesus Christ, it releases a grace. And it does seem from the feedback we get from all of them that they don't see Christians in a humble posture very often. So as we go in humility, they feel free to open their hearts to us immediately and we see things that are ordinarily hidden to the Christian among Muslims. For instance, not only do people open their hearts to us but we learn from them (we have so much to learn from them). We have begun to get a feel for what it is like to be a people who are feared and often the object of disdain from the West, a people who feel that they are constantly on the receiving end of Western power and authority. Whether that is military action, economic or cultural superiority, or even missionary superiority. Don't misunderstand, I believe that our message is relevant to them, but I've learned that oftentimes the lives we live are not worth displaying to them.[15]

Both the statement and Green's own reflection display the kind of disavowal of Constantine sought by Yoder, for although in many senses a grand gesture with international profile, it was in the local engagements with particular Muslim, Jewish and Orthodox communities that transformation took place, especially with Muslims. Green reflected on a meeting with a leading Shiite cleric in Lebanon:

Now, what would you expect a patriarch of the Shiite world to say to a group of Christians? After we read the statement of apology, he said, 'In Christian doctrine, Jesus came and sacrificed himself for all humanity. The cross has become the symbol therefore of self-denial and sacrifice. So when someone holds tightly to the cross, he is holding tightly to what this cross represents. There's a great deal of difference to what this cross represents and what it was used for in the Crusades. God sent his only son and sacrificed him for the whole of humanity. In the Crusades the cross was used for the way one human being terrorized another. Christianity means one word: love. Nowadays do we have love? Why did the Crusaders make us hate the one person who preached that love? As a Muslim following Muslim doctrine I am not considered a Muslim unless I believe in Jesus Christ. When I am taught to love Jesus Christ and everything he stands for, how can this stay in my heart when his followers do not live as they should? I feel that often I am more Christian than they are.'

And on encountering the care for the residents in a Muslim orphanage:

I remember when we met Mrs Rabab. She runs a fantastic orphanage, 300 girls. It's run so well, beautifully designed and built, immaculately clean, wonderful food, happy children and staff. And you think, my theology says this shouldn't be this way. This should be a legalistic and hard sort of place; the children's spirits being crushed. But it's not that way. I think I now feel a little of what Peter must have felt in Acts 10, when the Holy Spirit fell on Cornelius' house. At first, everybody said, 'It's not supposed to happen this way.' Finally Peter said, 'I now realize how true it is that God does not show favouritism but accepts men from every nation who fear him and do what is right' (Acts 10:34–35). I remember looking at Mrs Rabab and thinking: if ever there was a woman who fit this description, this is the woman. How many of these Muslims are there? We keep meeting them.

In a later talk given to Youth with a Mission volunteers in 2014,[16] Green reflects on an experience of meeting with Sufis attached to the lineage of Rumi and experiencing watching 'Whirling Dervishes'. He started by reflecting on how as an evangelical charismatic 'in touch with the spiritual world', his first response to the idea of such a thing was to dismiss it as demonic. However, he was moved by the sincerity and spiritual power of the event and felt that here were 'people of peace', as described by Jesus to his disciples.[17] In both the interview and in his storytelling to YWAM volunteers, Green wrestles with a theology that seeks to acknowledge the Spirit of Christ present in such Muslims while maintaining an evangelical integrity. It is a creative and thoughtful wrestling that draws on a conservative inclusive theology of religions and also 'insider movement'[18] missiology to explain what he experienced. However, more important than Green's missiological and pneumatological rationales for what he experienced, is what we witness in his narrative, in both the interview and talk: a sense of his own conversion to a deeper relationship with Christ in the process of opening to Muslims and discovering 'the presence of Christ' before him. Such an increased awareness leads to an ethical and practical approach to relationship with Christ as true witness and evangelism. He says:

Virtually no one takes exception to people who seek to follow the example of Jesus. The church for the first three centuries focused not so much on the finer points of doctrine but on following the commandments of Jesus. Living like that, they represented Jesus to a pagan world and the church grew at an incredible rate. It seems clear that if we don't seek to live like him people don't want to hear from us because they perceive the hypocrisy.

For some involved in the Walk of Reconciliation, the experience drew them ever more deeply into engaging in a radical work of reconciliation. One group established a missional community in Luton, a town with a significant Muslim community, and displayed a radical 'disavowal of Constantine' in their founding objectives:

TO AFFIRM that Jesus Christ is not the enemy of the peoples of the Middle East, to clarify his true nature to the peoples of the Middle East.

TO CHALLENGE ideologies and actions which confuse Christ with nationalism, political power, military power, or domination.

TO CHAMPION actions demonstrating the nature of Christ's non-worldly kingdom: acts of service in place of domination, and self-sacrifice in place of self-interest.

TO UNMASK mythologies of enmity that developed as a result of historical Christians who did not fulfil the vision of Christ's Kingdom, who instead acted as a self-interested, dominating, coercive worldly power.

TO HUMANIZE RELATIONSHIPS. Jesus Christ emphasized the value of humanity as created in the image of God. Humility and compassion toward one another preceded ideological, national or religious judgment in Christ's relationship models. He described authority that serves and dies for the human, rather than demanding that people serve a corporate hierarchy or ideology.[19]

The Reconciliation Walk demonstrates that a 'disavowal of Constantine' is not an act of weakness and denial of Christ in the face of the other but a witnessing to his peace and an opening of the disciple's heart to Christ who challenges us through encounter with the other into a deeper relationship with his call to peace.

A Parish and the 'War on Terror'

The concerns of this chapter arise out of my own personal journey and that of the church community for which I was parish priest between 1999 and 2007, engaging with Islam in the midst of the world events post the brutalities of 9/11 and 7/7 and the tyrannical response of the so-called 'war on terror', which I have written about elsewhere.[20] The context of this experience was a parish with a significant Muslim population and in which the bomb factory for the 7/7 bombers was discovered, at a location not 100 yards from the church. In our engagement, I felt we had been brought strongly into dialogue with the Yoderian exploration of the 'disavowal of Constantine'.[21]

My own personal journey – and to a degree that of the church community – in the midst of these political realities might be described as moving from Knitter's liberationist pluralism to a more Christological pacifism akin to Yoder. I have written elsewhere of how the radical Peace Church scholar Ched Myers' work on Mark's Gospel, *Binding the Strong Man*, helped root our community in the hope of Christ during our resistance to both war and the political despair prevalent in the secular anti-war movement with the onset of the invasion of Iraq:

> *Binding the Strong Man* has proved particularly important in rooting me in a gospel understanding of non-violence and resistance to empire since 9/11 and responding to the 'war on terror'. It influenced my contribution to my Christian Community at the time developing a militant non-violent witness to the so-called 'war on terror' from 2001 onwards. The idea of Mark's community being one that saw Jesus' call as one to non-violent direct action but also one that refused to demonize the opposition and also cautioned against the search

for direct historical efficacy to one's resistance was significant on two counts – first speaking to our experience of marginalization in our public resistance as a church community to the war on Afghanistan and the division that created within our own community and second in the light of the failure of resistance to the war on Iraq 'succeeding'. My call for our community to organize an anti-war event after the invasion of Iraq was deeply influenced by this understanding of the call of Jesus Christ to a certain kind of resistance rooted in what Ched called 'revolutionary patience'.[22]

However, while I increasingly experienced the spiritual empowerment inherent in a tradition-specific commitment to Christological non-violence, I believe I also wanted to develop an understanding that Christological non-violence is enhanced and indeed deepened through serious encounter and dialogue with other faith traditions, which is affirmed in Knitter's pluralism. I would want to argue that the Christological non-violence aligned to an approach to other faiths that is kenotic in its Christian particularity – focusing on an ethical reading of the Philippians hymn for the Christian in their discipleship in the world – calls for a deep encounter with the religious other and for Christian particularity itself to be formed by that encounter. It is interesting that elsewhere in his writings, Yoder calls for such an ethical understanding of Philippians 2. In a recent analysis of Yoder's work, including unpublished lectures, J. Denny Weaver has argued that, rather than seeing Philippians 2 as describing Jesus' metaphysical descent from his divine nature giving up 'equality with God' in order to become human and then through his obedience being raised to his original exalted state, Yoder saw in Philippians 2 a 'second Adam' Christology in which:

[The term] 'image of God' makes Jesus parallel to Adam, who was created in the image of God. But from that status, Adam tried to grasp equality with God. In contrast Jesus continued as the 'model of what Adam should have done, refusing to seize that which was not his.' This later interpretation keeps in view the full humanity of Jesus, 'even to the point of death.'

Jesus is then given the title of Lord because of this complete and perfect obedience . . . Believers are called to imitate the humility of Jesus . . . that humility becomes the basis of unity. Unity requires the respect for the other person, which is based on following the example of Christ who humbled himself. The ultimate result will then be being raised with Christ.[23]

Returning to Yoder's 1976 essay noted above, we see expressed here a willingness to be open to the other and allow the pull of the other's faith to have an impact on us, and he argues for a necessary understanding of mission and dialogue that recognizes that the pull of the other's tradition and the urge to share my own are part of the same dynamic, but that this is worked out in the particular and local engagements in relationship between adherents of different traditions rather than through representational engagements between the institutions and establishments or theological 'answers' such as 'Anonymous Christianity'. In this engagement, a double vulnerability is asserted by Yoder in which living the truth of Jesus' non-violent witness enables the Christian to be vulnerable to the attraction and the dignity of the other in their culture and conviction.

> Thus defined, the kerygmatic truth claim stands in no tension with a posture of dialogue that affirms fully the dignity of the interlocutor, including his or her culture and conviction. But it can only be distinguished from the colonial or Crusader truth claim if the herald's double vulnerability is clearly perceived and willingly affirmed.[24]

Interestingly, Hauerwas has reflected on the need to understand Christian pacifism in a deeper sense that involves more than merely the resistance of war, but displays qualities of vulnerability and openness to others, to shape us and challenge us. He says:

> I hate the language of pacifism because it is too passive. But by avowing it, I create expectations in others that hopefully will help me live faithfully to what I know is true but that I have no confidence in my own ability to live it at all. That's part of

what non-violence is – the attempt to make our lives vulnerable to others in a way that we need one another. To be against war – which is clearly violent – is a good place to start. But you never know where the violence is in your own life. To say you're non-violent is not some position of self-righteousness – you kill and I don't. It's rather to make your life available to others in a way that they can help you discover ways you're implicated in violence you hadn't even noticed.[25]

Taking Hauerwas' statement alongside Yoder's call for a deep engagement with a process of the disavowal of Constantine, we are led perhaps to a practice that seeks to analyse how the violence of the Constantinian models of church lives on in Christian missiology and engagement with others of different faiths.

The missiologist Martha Frederiks has identified five models of Christian missiology in relationship to other faiths:

1 Expansion – concentrating on the conversion of people of other faiths to Christianity.
2 Diakonia or service – providing services such as schools, hospitals.
3 Presence – simply living among people of other faiths and being in solidarity with them.
4 Dialogue – engaging in respectful conversations and explorations of each other's faiths.
5 Kenosis – placing at the centre a Christological understanding of our relationship to people of other faiths located in the idea of a kenotic relationship of vulnerability to others.[26]

Bringing each of these models under the light of Yoder's critique of Constantinianism and Hauerwas' call for an understanding of Christian pacifism that is open to our practices of hidden violence being critiqued and exposed through a non-violent vulnerability in relation to the other, we could reflect on which models deepen our engagement with the particularity of Christological non-violence.

It could be argued that the Expansion model of seeing mission as converting people from other faiths to Christianity purely for purposes of expansion and control prevalent throughout church history is firmly rooted in a Constantinian model and displays collaboration with both overt and covert forms of violence. And while the service-led approach of Diakonia – again a feature of the Western missionary movement – might be seen as a development away from a crude expansionist model, it still views service as a way towards expansion, concentrating on service to the religious other in order to attract and convert, and therefore still needs to be seen in the light of Yoder's analysis, as rooted in a Constantinian model, particularly as practitioners of this model have often made no attempt to subvert the power dynamics between rich and poor and indeed often reinforced them through relationships of dependence. Where it has begun to address issues of inequality it has tended to become de-Christianized in favour of a liberal universalism that in itself poses dangers of hidden violence.

The Dialogue model is a product of the late twentieth century, and an increasing Western consciousness of the reality of pluralism raises again questions of power, as Tinu Ruparell has pointed out:

> At least one major impetus for interreligious dialogue is suspect. Our colonialist guilt brings with it a form of dialogue built on false, ideological egalitarianism which homogenizes people and ironically further supports the inequalities and injustices wrought by the history of colonialism in the first place.[27]

Present in each of these models, it might be argued, is a potential towards 'violence' in some form, a potential towards Constantinian models of church. This leaves the Presence and Kenosis models as more fitting to an approach to engagement based on Christological non-violence. Frederiks sees the Presence model as going back to the work of St Francis of Assisi, particularly in relation to Islam, as outlined by Franciscan scholars in recent years,[28] in the work of missionaries like Max Warren and Roger Hooker[29] and also present in a more politicized and radical form – and in a different context – in the worker-priest movement in France in the 1950s and 1960s, a model of presence that required a 'subversion of the status quo'.[30] Presence as a model for Christian encounter with other faiths could be seen as requiring serious engagement with the religious other on their terms and joining with the other in solidarity, again on their terms and their agenda rather than a generalized global ethic, acting and relating out of the 'disavowal' called for by Yoder to challenge actions of society that had a negative impact on our neighbours of other traditions. This is radicalized further in the model of Kenosis, which has the added advantage of being firmly rooted in a Christological paradigm and developing the potentially positive elements of diakonia and dialogue in more securely Christological directions, free of the tendencies to forms of Constantinian violence. Frederiks writes:

> The model sees radical self-emptying as a necessity to establishing meaningful relationships with people of other faiths . . . It is only in true and radical openness to the other in the totally of his/her being and openness to his/her deepest motivations in life, that the witness of God's love for all people can be shared. Inculturation and interreligious dialogue therefore are not just optional for the interested few, but, according to the model of kenosis, they belong to the core of the Christian calling to imitate Christ in his self-emptying love for people. They are authentic expressions of the Christian identity.[31]

St Francis and Damietta – The Development of Presence Ministry – A Case Study in Conversion[32]

When Pope Innocent III launched his campaign for a Fifth Crusade in 1213, in order to recapture Jerusalem from the control of Islam, the whole of the Christian Church in Europe was recruited to the cause and it became a central feature of church life. Crusade preachers were commissioned, special prayers added to the liturgy and sacrificial financial giving encouraged. The Crusades were organized under the slogan *Deus vult*, 'God wills it', and St Bernard was not unusual in his attitude that 'to kill a Muslim is not murder'. After Innocent died in 1216, while touring to drum up support for the Crusade, Pope Honorius III replaced him and on his inauguration issued a fresh call for the whole of Christendom to become involved in raising money and in praying for a new Crusade. He added a large degree of moral pressure when he wrote that those who did not put their names to a Crusade were guilty of 'the vice of ingratitude and the crime of infidelity'.

However, Francis appears not to have reflected on this decree, or on any decrees making reference to the Crusades, although he wrote to his brothers in the Franciscan order about most papal documents of the time, including significant decrees on the Eucharist and penance. Neither is there any record of the Franciscans participating in this campaign in any way, including the call for special prayers and acts of penance to receive God's blessing on the endeavour. Franciscan historians have reflected on this, and concluded that St Francis and the brothers chose to resist the call to crusade by non-compliance with the campaign, which they saw as a denial of, rather than a witness to, the gospel.

Francis went even further when the Crusade was actually launched – he sought to persuade the Pope to have a change of heart. When that failed he travelled to Egypt himself, to where the Crusaders were laying siege to the city of Damietta, and attempted to persuade the Christian commander, Cardinal Pelagius, to end the fighting. When he refused, Francis crossed over to the other side and sought an audience with the Muslim leader, Sultan Malik al-Kamil. He wanted to let the Sultan know that the Crusaders did not represent, in their violence and warmongering, the true spirit of Jesus Christ. He wanted to give witness to God's love in Jesus Christ. In his biography of St Francis, St Bonaventure wrote of the event:

> The sultan asked them by whom and why and in what capacity they had been sent, and how they got there; but Francis replied intrepidly that they had been sent by God, not by man, to show him and his subjects the way of salvation and proclaim the truth of the gospel message.
>
> When the sultan saw his enthusiasm and courage, he listened to him willingly and pressed him to stay with him . . .

then he offered Francis a number of valuable presents, but the saint was anxious only for the salvation of souls, he had no interest in the things of the earth and so he scorned them all as if they were so much dust. The sultan was lost in admiration at the sight of such perfect disregard for worldly wealth and he felt greater respect than ever for the saint.

Francis went to Egypt longing to bring the Crusaders to repentance and, through his peaceful and risky witness, the Muslims to a Christian belief in Jesus as Saviour. He seems to have failed on both accounts. But if he held on to the powerful sense of being sent by God, did he come to an understanding that it was *he* who was converted to a deeper understanding of God in the process? Arising out of a living, loving witness comes an openness to the Muslim faith and Islam as a spiritual path, and an ability to learn and grow in understanding of God through the process of encounter and witness.

Some contemporary commentators have argued that during his time in the Middle East, Francis was affected by what he saw of the practice of Islam. Some time after Francis returned to Italy, he wrote his 'Letter to the Rulers of the People', in which he instructs them, maybe having been influenced by the Adhan, the Call to Prayer:

> See to it that God is held in great reverence among your subjects; every evening, at a signal given by a herald or in some other way, praise and thanks should be given to the Lord God Almighty by all the people.

He was also apparently influenced by the practice of prostration in Muslim prayers. In his 'Letter to a General Chapter of the Franciscans' he writes: 'At the sound of God's name you should fall to the ground and adore him with fear and reverence.'

The reason friars are sent all over the world, he adds, is to 'bear witness . . . that there is no other Almighty God besides him', echoing the Muslim *Shahada*: 'There is no god but God!' Some have argued that some of Francis' later prayers were influenced by his contact with the Muslim practice of reciting the 99 names of God, including The Gracious, The Kindly, The Beneficent,

The High One, The Merciful, The Compassionate, The Mighty, The Loving . . . Francis' prayer 'The Praises of God' could well have been influenced by this aspect of Islamic spirituality:

You are holy, Lord, the only God, and Your deeds are wonderful.
You are strong.
You are great.
You are the Most High.
You are Almighty.
You, Holy Father, are King of heaven and earth.
You are Three and One,
Lord God, all Good,
You are Good, all Good, supreme Good,
Lord God, living and true.
You are love.
You are wisdom.
You are humility.
You are endurance.
You are rest.
You are peace.
You are joy and gladness.
You are justice and moderation.

You are all our riches.
And You suffice for us.
You are beauty.
You are gentleness.
You are our protector.
You are our guardian and defender.
You are courage.
You are our haven and our hope.
You are our faith,
our great consolation.
You are our eternal life,
Great and Wonderful Lord,
God Almighty,
Merciful Saviour.
Amen

Did this seeming influence of Islamic spirituality on his own prayer life signify a greater appreciation for the presence of God in Islam? In his last draft of the rule of the Order, Francis recommends that brothers be allowed to minister among Muslims. He prioritizes a mission and witness of loving action over direct proselytization, insisting they avoid quarrels and disputation with Muslims and work at acts of service and love relating to all human beings. Only after doing this, 'if it pleases God', are they to preach the faith in words.

Kenosis as Corrective to Pluralism and Particularism

This process of kenosis outlined by Frederiks overcomes the dangers of 'sectarianism' in relation to other faiths often attributed to the 'new traditionalists', by their critics and often presented as an argument against particularism in theology of religions by pluralists.[33] It also avoids the oppressive universalizing tendencies of the liberationist pluralism of Knitter through rooting the mode of encounter firmly within Christian practices of non-violence, to the point that on occasion Christian particularity requires that a step into the particularity of the other is required in order to be truly non-violent and remain true to that very Christian particularity. The search is not for a common ethic or practice but for the Christian, through a practice rooted in the engagement with the other in relation to the realities of a suffering and struggling world awaiting its eschatological fulfilment, to live non-defensively and in so doing to practise a Christian discipleship in the reality of a multifaith world that – in the particular context of my parish mentioned above, of Christians relating to their Muslim neighbours – resists the 'war on terror' with a Christian practice of non-violence in relation to Islam that is rooted in the spiritual practice of kenosis, the fruits of which are repentance, conversion and sanctification of the Christian community themselves.

This practice of non-violence is not rooted in an 'absolutist pacifism' drawn from an external philosophy of non-violence but is rooted in an understanding of a disciple's experience of resurrection, what the Catholic activist theologian Daniel Berrigan has called an 'ethic of resurrection'. Berrigan, perhaps best known for his resistance to the Vietnam War and for the Trident ploughshares movement, is keen to point out that:

> This is our glory. From Peter and Paul to Martin King and Romero, Christians have known something which the 'nations' as such can never know or teach – how to live and how to die. We are witnesses of the resurrection. We practice resurrection. We risk resurrection.[34]

Non-violence is therefore neither a tactic nor an absolutist principle but an experiencing of the resurrection, a living of our baptism; and we are called to take that deeply as part of a spiritual journey and praxis, to resist war, yes, but also to open our own hearts to where the forces of death still work within us in the hidden violence of our attitudes to others, including other faith traditions. To do so is to live in Christ and to deepen our *Christian* spirituality. The ethic of resurrection enables an ethic of kenosis and the disciples' transformation.

Interfaith Engagement as a 'Means of Grace'

It is here that we might bring in understandings of holiness and what the eighteenth-century revivalist John Wesley termed the 'way of salvation'. In the very engagement with the call to a Christological non-violence at its deepest level in relation to other faith traditions, the Christian community and the individual disciple experience the grace of God working in their lives. This grace works in such a way that one might argue that other faith traditions are not simply, in the liberationist's understanding, partners for developing a global ethic, but a means of grace, through which God sanctifies the Christian and makes the understanding of the work that has been done in Christ for her benefit an experiential reality that, in turn, continues to perfect her in her growth into living the love of God through developing the mind of Christ.

Wesley's theology was an experientially verified theology that sought to know the reality of Christ's saving work in the Christian. This was to be experienced and the process of this experiencing and knowing was the order or way of salvation. Wesley's understanding, influenced by his contact with Moravians, sought to develop Arminian over Calvinist approaches in the eighteenth-century evangelical revival that asserted free will and rejected predestination, arguing that knowledge of one's salvation can be experienced. Equally against Calvinism, human sinfulness did not lead to total depravity but to human deprivation of the knowledge of our true self in relation to God. But that deprivation, although marring the image of God in us, remains divine in its orientation and open to what Wesley called 'prevenient' or 'convicting' grace that enables us to understand our condition and seek repentance. The Holy Spirit works through the image of God in us to encourage us to act out of our free will to respond to prevenient or convicting grace. In the seeking of repentance in response to this we experience justification – a knowledge of God's forgiveness – and in living in the light of that knowledge we grow in holiness through justifying grace and experience assurance through a process of sanctifying grace that gives us a deeper understanding of Christ's love and power in our lives and enables us to live that love, becoming 'perfected' in the process. This threefold movement is dynamic and a process of growth and transformation – this for Wesley is salvation.

> What is salvation? The salvation which is here spoken of is not what is frequently understood by that word, the going to heaven, eternal happiness . . . it is not a blessing which lies on the other side of death, or (as we usually speak) in the other world . . . It is a present thing, a blessing which, through the free mercy of God, ye are now in possession of.[35]

But what is equally important to understand is that this process can be and needs to be encouraged and enabled through practices that open us to the grace of God at work in the world. This was the thrust of Wesley's movement and message. Knight lists these 'means of grace' into three categories that include activities such as prayer, keeping the Commandments, doing no harm, searching the Scriptures, the Lord's supper, fasting and abstinence, among others.[36] It is here that our understanding of interfaith encounter as a spiritual practice – as a means of grace – comes into being; our encounter with other faith traditions is a continual opportunity to grow into the love of God. Through our dynamic interaction we can experience in our encounter with the other a prevenient and convicting grace that draws us to recognize our sin as a church. This is Yoder's 'disavowal of Constantine', our recognition of the need of repentance for having not lived the love of Christ. In opening our heart to our own sinfulness in relation to the other and to Christ, we can be transformed into a deeper understanding of God's forgiveness for us. Thus, through our non-violent engagement with the other in whom Christ meets us, we find ourselves less defensive in relation to the other and able to open our hearts to the sanctifying grace that helps us to perfect ourselves in love, growing more deeply through the challenge of encounter into the mind of Christ. And this is a 'means of grace' – in a deeply non-violent approach to other faiths we are experiencing the way of salvation. Then encounter itself becomes a means of grace and a justifying and sanctifying process – we grow in our knowledge of Christ and our practice of Love. We are drawn to repentance, are deepened in our faith and grow in holiness. This process can clearly be seen to be at work and is a way of understanding the experiences, both of the Walk of Reconciliation and of St Francis' trip to Damietta.

It was after his Aldersgate experience that Wesley began to understand and develop his thinking on the way of salvation. Central, as has been said, was his understanding of this as an experiential reality. Justification was, for Wesley, an experience known spiritually, not just intellectually, and his Aldersgate experience was interpreted as such an encounter. In his journal he wrote:

In the evening, I went very unwillingly to a society in Aldersgate Street, where one was reading Luther's preface to the Epistle to the Romans. About a quarter before nine, while he was describing the change which God works in the heart through faith in Christ, I felt my heart strangely warmed. I felt I did trust in Christ, Christ alone, for salvation; and an assurance was given me that He had taken away my sins, even mine, and saved me from the law of sin and death. I began to pray with all my might for those who had in a more especial manner despitefully used me and persecuted me. I then testified openly to all there what I now first felt in my heart.[37]

Wesley sought to explore how the way of salvation was truly experienced by the early Methodists, and the impact on that experience of the means of grace. In emphasizing the experiential reality of God's saving work in the Christian, Wesley drives us to a narrative theology that seeks to articulate the reality of God's saving work through the exploration of our experience. In relation to the assertion of God's grace being communicated to us through our relationship to other faith traditions, we need a qualitative examination of examples of Christian encounter. We have begun this in this chapter with examination of two case studies of Christian engagement with Islam represented by the Walk of Reconciliation and recent Franciscan scholarship on St Francis' encounter with Islam during the Crusades. We will continue the examination below in a third case study rooted in my own community's engagement with the 'war on terror'. Wesley's threefold understanding of salvation is the interpretative framework by which I seek to understand the experiences of challenge, conflict, joy and spiritual renewal experienced in these stories. In engaging with Wesley's threefold understanding of the dynamics of the Christian experience of grace, I read this not exclusively as a linear progression but as a dynamic spiral of experience in which the threefold understanding of the experience of the Christian described either as repentance, faith and holiness or conviction, justification and sanctification are for ever more deeply encountered in the growth into the perfecting love of God. As Cracknell has pointed out when referring to the experience of prevenient grace (often seen in Wesleyan understanding as the grace that prompts response to God and the developing awareness of our sin and need for repentance):

'Prevenience' is not a stage of grace, some part of a putative Wesleyan order of salvation (first prevenient grace, then real grace!), but is rather the crucial aspect of grace in all its manifestations. It signifies the divine initiative in all spirituality, in all Christian experience, among all people. It is at once the work of Christ and the work of the Spirit.[38]

I am not claiming that this interpretation would necessarily meet with John Wesley's approval. Although portraying particularly negative views on Islam, Wesley often used the encounter with Islam for reflection on the failings of nominal Christianity.[39] However, my purposes here are to utilize Wesley's understanding of the Christian spiritual journey in dialogue with Yoder's Christological non-violence as a way of exploring the potential power of interfaith encounter on Christians. Interfaith encounter, rather than taking the Christian away from their particularity in Christ, takes them, I would want to argue, into a deeper and sanctifying experience in which that very particularity is enhanced in the process of risking it through a non-violent kenotic defencelessness.

Open to Islam Open to Christ – A Case Study in Sanctification

As mentioned in a previous chapter, in 2005 I undertook the Ramadan fast as fully as possible and engaged with the Qur'an. The following is taken from my spiritual diary of the time and is an example of how opening to the riches of another tradition helps to deepen the process of engagement with one's own tradition's truth and live it more fully. This might traditionally be called sanctification, a process leading to an engagement with an understanding of Islam – peace through submission to God – that helps reengagement with Paul's kenotic hymn in Philippians 2 and through that, a kenotic interpretation of the praxis of the beatitudes. The following are reflections from the journal.

This morning's reading from the Qur'an was interesting:

O ye who believe!
Cancel not your charity
By reminders of your generosity
Or by injury – like those
Who spend their wealth
To be seen by men,
But believe neither
In Allah nor in the last day.
They are in parable like a hard,
Barren rock, on which
Is a little soil: on it
Falls heavy rain.
Which leaves it
A bare stone.
They will be able to do nothing

With aught they have earned
And Allah guideth not
Those who reject faith.
And the likeness of those
Who spend their wealth
Seeking to please Allah
And to strengthen their souls,
Is a garden, high
And fertile: heavy rain
Falls on it but makes it yield
A double increase
Of harvest, and if it receives not
Heavy rain, light moisture
Sufficeth it. Allah seeth well
Whatever ye do.

It seems that the fertility that comes from submission to God is an inner growth, a strengthening of the soul. Really feeling attracted to this idea of submission, something I would have found oppressive in the past, but am feeling a sense of joy at the submission of my will to God, a letting go of control and a giving oneself over through practice of prayer, fasting and seeking more simplicity: spending wealth seeking to please Allah. This idea of submission in Islam is powerful and beautiful to me . . . I learn more and more from Islam the need for submission, the need to strip myself of belief in my own power and control. I see that is Islam's gift – the call to submission:

> If anyone desires
> A religion other than Islam (submission to Allah)
> Never will it be accepted of him; and in the Hereafter
> He will be in the ranks
> Of those who have lost.

As a Christian my submission to Allah is through Christ; I seek therefore an Islamic Christianity. Christ, it appears to me, is the true Muslim, the one who submitted most fully to God's will. As St Paul says, quoting an early Christian hymn:

> He humbled himself and became obedient to the point of death – even death on a cross. Therefore God also highly exalted him and gave him the name that is above every name, so that at the name of Jesus every knee should bend, in heaven and on earth and under the earth, and every tongue should confess that Jesus Christ is Lord, to the glory of God the Father.

It seems to me that the call to submission is a call to peace. It is our desire for control and power – our desire to be gods – that leads to violence on all levels. It is the call to submission to God that is at the heart of Jesus' Beatitudes. The Beatitudes call us to let go of control and pride and to really be humble. To be empowered by a knowledge of God to whom we submit our desires for control, wealth and success and instead display the truth about our yearning for Spirit, our sadness at our own and the world's shortcomings and the seeming rule of death, our smallness in the great scheme of things, our longing for right to be done beyond political agendas; practising mercy, forgiveness, letting go. Seeking holiness, purity of heart where desire becomes wrapped totally in love rather than lust and power, and living in a way that by just being we are peacemakers in the everyday; and finally accepting as our lot, at best marginality, at worst direct persecution.

> Blessed are the poor in spirit, for theirs is the kingdom of heaven.
> Blessed are those who mourn, for they will be comforted.
> Blessed are the meek, for they will inherit the earth.
> Blessed are those who hunger and thirst for righteousness, for they will be filled.
> Blessed are the merciful, for they will receive mercy.
> Blessed are the pure in heart, for they will see God.
> Blessed are the peacemakers, for they will be called children of God.
> Blessed are those who are persecuted for righteousness' sake, for theirs is the kingdom of heaven.
> Blessed are you when people revile you and persecute you and utter all kinds of evil against you falsely on my account. Rejoice and be glad, for your reward is great in heaven, for in the same way they persecuted the prophets who were before you.

Conclusion

What I hope I have tentatively outlined in this chapter is a theology of interfaith engagement that is rooted in a creative engagement with the Peace Church tradition of the radical reformation and the Wesleyan revivalist tradition of eighteenth-century evangelicalism, what might be termed a radical revivalist theology of interfaith engagement, which perhaps encourages us to see such engagement as an opportunity for Christian renewal. Recently both the Methodist and Anglican Churches in England, with which I am involved, have been concerned about decline and the need for growth. At such a time the temptation is to see interfaith engagement as a peripheral issue or people of other faiths as potential conversion fodder, highlighting the small number of conversions that actually take place across traditions, or to see other faiths as competitors in the market place, adopting aggressively apologetic stances as religion becomes increasingly commodified in our consumerist culture.

I want us to take another path. The Archbishop of Canterbury has listed three priorities for the Church of England in the coming period: spiritual renewal; reconciliation; evangelism and witness. My understanding is that interfaith engagement is crucial to the first two – our own spiritual renewal and developing a deeper understanding of Christ's reconciling work come through interfaith engagement, and the above reflections assert that. The third arises out of the first two and happens not through targets and strategies and developing a new 'expansionist' model of mission but as the outworking of our increased holiness as we deepen our relationship to Christ through our creative encounter with those of other faiths based on a kenotic defencelessness and an active and prayerful engagement with the experiential reality of our own salvation.

'Let the same mind be in you that was in Christ Jesus', says Paul in the letter to the Philippians, and 'work out your own salvation with fear and trembling; for it is God who is at work in you, enabling you both to will and to work for his good pleasure' (Philippians 2.5, 12b–13).

Notes

1 Paul F. Knitter, 'Is the Pluralist Model a Western Imposition?', in Paul F. Knitter (ed.), *The Myth of Religious Superiority: Multifaith Explorations of Religious Pluralism* (Maryknoll, NY: Orbis, 2005), p. 40.

2 Stanley Hauerwas, *Performing the Faith: Bonhoeffer and the Practice of Nonviolence* (Grand Rapids, MI: Brazos, 2004), p. 26.

3 Paul F. Knitter, *One Earth, Many Religions: Multifaith Dialogue and Global Responsibility* (Maryknoll, NY: Orbis, 1995).

4 Jeffrey Stout, *Democracy and Tradition* (Princeton, NJ: Princeton University Press, 2004), pp. 118ff.

5 Gavin D'Costa, *The Meeting of Religions and the Trinity* (Maryknoll, NY: Orbis, 2000), pp. 30–40.

6 Stanley Hauerwas, 'The End of "Religious Pluralism"', in *The State of the University: Academic Knowledges and the Knowledge of God* (Oxford: Blackwell, 2007), pp. 58–75.

7 After I had started this exploration I became aware of the widespread abuse that John Howard Yoder had perpetrated over a number of years and the campaign by survivors and others within the Mennonite Church for acknowledgement of that abuse to be taken seriously and to reveal the complicity of church authorities with it over years. I publish links here to articles exploring this in an edition of the *Mennonite Quarterly* review: https://themennonite.org/feature/failure-bind-loose-responses-john -howard-yoders-sexual-abuse. Questions about the use of Yoder's material in the light of these findings are explored in J. Denny Weaver (ed.), *John Howard Yoder: Radical Theologian* (Eugene, OR: Cascade, 2014).

8 John Howard Yoder, 'The Disavowal of Constantine: An Alternative Perspective on Interfaith Dialogue', in John Howard Yoder, *The Royal Priesthood: Essays Ecclesiological and Ecumenical*, ed. Michael G. Cartwright (Grand Rapids, MI: Eerdmans, 1994), pp. 242–61.

9 John Howard Yoder, *The Politics of Jesus*, 2nd edn (Carlisle: Paternoster, 1993).

10 John Howard Yoder, *The Jewish–Christian Schism Revisited*, ed. Michael G. Cartwright and Peter Ochs (London: SCM Press, 2003).

11 Paul F. Knitter, *Jesus and the Other Names: Christian Mission and Global Responsibility* (Oxford: Oneworld, 1996).

12 See essays in Gavin D'Costa (ed.), *Christian Uniqueness Reconsidered: The Myth of a Pluralistic Theology of Religions* (Maryknoll, NY: Orbis, 1990).

13 Yoder, *Royal Priesthood*, pp. 250–1.

14 See www.recwalk.net.

15 Lynn Green interviewed by Charles Strohmer for *Openings #3* (April–June 1999); edited version at www.charlesstrohmer.com/writings/interviews /lynn-green-muslims-christians.

16 See *The Reconciliation Walk: God Stories with Lynn Green*. Youth With A Mission videos on YouTube, in three parts, at www.youtube .com/watch?v=RgthDbxAOVg and www.youtube.com/watch?v=1429y is1uNo&t=5s and www.youtube.com/watch?v=VkTzx59xn88 (accessed 1/3/2017).

17 See Luke 9 and 10.

18 For exploration of the 'insider movement', see *The International Journal of Frontier Missions* 17:1 (2000).

19 Website of Reconciliation Walk – www.recwalk.net (accessed 8/11/16).

20 Ray Gaston, *A Heart Broken Open: Radical Faith in an Age of Fear* (Glasgow: Wild Goose Publications, 2009).

21 Richard Lock-Pullan identifies the position of All Hallows at the time as influenced by and similar to postliberal theologians such as Cavanagh and Hauerwas – see Richard Lock-Pullan, 'The Church and the War on Terror', in Timothy Blewett, Adrian Hyde-Price and Wyn Rees (eds), *British Foreign Policy and the Anglican Church: Christian*

Engagement with the Contemporary World (Aldershot: Ashgate, 2008), pp. 101–3.

22 Ray Gaston, quoted in the Introduction to Ched Myers' Anniversary Edition, *Binding the Strong Man: A Political Reading of Mark's Story of Jesus* (Maryknoll, NY: Orbis, 2008), p. li.

23 Weaver (ed.), *John Howard Yoder*, pp. 32–3.

24 Yoder, 'Disavowal of Constantine', p. 256.

25 Stanley Hauerwas, from an interview with Colman McCarthy in *The Progressive* (April 2003).

26 See Martha Th. Frederiks, 'Kenosis as a Model for Interreligious Dialogue' – www.missionstudies.org/archive/conference/1papers/fp/Martha _Frederiks_Full_paper.pdf (accessed 10/11/16).

27 Tinu Ruparell, 'The Dialogue Party: Dialogue, Hybridity, and the Reluctant Other', in Viggo Mortensen (ed.), *Theology and the Religions: A Dialogue* (Grand Rapids, MI: Eerdmans, 2003), p. 238.

28 J. Hoeberichts, *Francis and Islam* (Quincy, IL: Franciscan Press, 1997).

29 Graham Kings, *Christianity Connected: Hindus, Muslims and the World in the Letters of Max Warren and Roger Hooker* (Zoetermeer: Boekencentrum, 2002).

30 A model that also had followers in UK – see John Mantle, *Britain's First Worker-Priests: Radical Ministry in a Post-War Setting* (London: SCM Press, 2000).

31 Fredericks, 'Kenosis as a Model for Interreligious Dialogue', p. 11.

32 Much of the material in this section is drawn from two sources: Hoeberichts, *Francis and Islam* and Leonhard Lehmann, 'Francis' Two Letters to the Custodes: Proposals for Christian–Islamic Ecumenism in Praising God', *Greyfriars Review* 2:3 (1988), pp. 63–91.

33 James M. Gustafson, 'The Sectarian Temptation: Reflections on Theology, the Church and the University', *Proceedings of the Catholic Theological Society of America* 40 (1985), pp. 83–94.

34 Daniel Berrigan, *Testimony: The Word Made Flesh* (Maryknoll, NY: Orbis, 2004), p. 223.

35 *The Sermons of John Wesley*, Sermon 43, 'The Scripture Way of Salvation' – see http://wesley.nnu.edu/john-wesley/the-sermons-of-john -wesley-1872-edition/sermon-43-the-scripture-way-of-salvation.

36 Henry H. Knight, *The Presence of God in the Christian Life: John Wesley and the Means of Grace* (Metuchen, NJ: Scarecrow Press, 1992).

37 *Journal of John Wesley*, online at https://www.ccel.org/ccel/wesley/ journal.vi.ii.xvi.html (accessed 1/8/17).

38 Kenneth Cracknell, *Our Doctrines: Methodist Theology as Classical Christianity* (Calver: Cliff College, 1998), p. 64.

39 See Kenneth J. Collins, *The Theology of John Wesley: Holy Love and the Shape of Grace* (Nashville, TN: Abingdon Press, 2007), pp. 113–20.

PART 2

Challenging Islamophobia, Affirming Multiculturalism

4

Challenging Islamophobia

A Practical Theological Reflection

Introduction

A 2011 survey into anti-Muslim hate crime made disturbing reading. In their introduction, the authors affirmed my own experience on the ground as a parish priest in North West Leeds,[1] that incidents of such crimes rose following the US and UK response to the atrocity of 9/11. They highlighted an example from their survey of one incident from a catalogue of such everyday abuses experienced by some Muslims. Recounting the story of a young girl who witnessed her mother being punched because she was wearing a Niqab, the writers reflected on the effect on the girl and her mother:

> This particular incident is . . . illustrative of a widespread hidden experience for three reasons: first, the victim did not report the assault to police and did not discuss it outside of a close circle of family and friends; second, after the assault the victim reduced her travel by foot and by public transport to a minimum; third, neither victim, nor her family or friends had any inclination to address the causes of the attack but chose instead to retreat into the safety of a small network of trusted Muslim friends.[2]

However, incidents like the attack mentioned above, showing Muslims as victims of violence and prejudice, feature less in public discourse than opinions that generate and emphasize Islam as a 'dangerous other'. Writing in 2008 in the *Daily Telegraph*, the then Bishop of Rochester, Michael Nazir-Ali, claimed that parts of Britain's inner cities were 'no-go' areas where 'Islamic extremism' was 'a mark of acceptability':

> there has been a worldwide resurgence of the ideology of Islamic extremism. One of the results of this has been to further alienate the young from the nation in which they were growing up and also to turn already separate communities into 'no-go' areas where adherence to this ideology has become a mark of acceptability. Those of a different faith or race may find it difficult to live or work there because of hostility to them and even the risk of violence.[3]

However, the threat of violence is more a reality for Muslims as a minority within wider society than to non-Muslims living in 'Muslim areas'. It might be argued that the bishop's comments and other similar sentiments place Muslim communities in a 'double bind'. Prejudice encourages isolation and then Muslims are blamed for creating areas of safety and identity in a hostile society. In fact there is evidence to suggest a contrary movement, with remarkable levels of positive identification and integration among Muslim communities with British society,[4] despite evidence of growing Islamophobia.[5]

Islamophobia

Islamophobia, a contemporary term that first entered public discourse through the Runnymede Trust's report in 1997, is a phenomenon that has recently come under close academic scrutiny. The report described it as 'an unfounded hostility' towards Islam and Muslims.[6] A plethora of recent publications have explored its nature and whether it is a new phenomenon or simply the re-emergence of anti-Muslim prejudice that dates back to the medieval period and the Crusades. While the Runnymede Trust's original definition has been critiqued,[7] the usefulness of the concept in exploring a real social phenomenon continues to be advanced. According to one academic review of recent material, the concept of Islamophobia has 'come of age'.[8] The sociologist Tahir Abbas says: 'Islamophobia is a complex, multifaceted, economic, political, and cultural phenomenon, and its impact on Muslim/non-Muslim relations will remain an important feature of social life in Britain for some time.'[9]

On the ground in communities, the necessity to respond to a sense of increasing anti-Muslim hate crime has given rise to the 'Tell MAMA' initiative, which seeks to report cases of abuse and has produced, in cooperation with academics, a number of reports exploring the problem.[10] Associated with this rise in hate crime towards Muslims was the increased profile, from 2009 onwards, of a populist right-wing movement called the English Defence League (EDL). The EDL has been seen by some as an example of 'cumulative extremism',[11] given the movement's beginnings in response to demonstrations by the now proscribed 'Islam4UK' group. Cumulative extremism,[12] the idea that opposing 'extremist' groups feed off each other, is an interesting one; however, it is also important to link the EDL's rise to a heightened propagation of a 'clash of civilizations' thesis[13] that lay behind much of the rhetoric of the 'war on terror' after 2001. This claims there is a growing conflict and incompatibility between 'Islam' and 'the West' and could be argued to be at the core of Islamophobic discourse. It has been shown by Richardson, in his comparative analysis of Muslims in media election coverage of the elections of 1997, 2001 and 2005,[14] that the examples of rising hostility to Muslims and Islam in the press served:

> the very practical function of removing British Muslims from empowered positions in and affecting the public sphere by demanding either their cultural and political assimilation or expulsion. It should be viewed as an example of a 'discourse of spatial management', founded on the 'white fantasy' of the journalists and readers, according to which they have the right and ability to regulate the ethnic and religious parameters of British society.[15]

The English Defence League as an Islamophobic Movement

Despite proven links to the far right, the EDL's support was developed not by traditional far-right politics but by a deeply Islamophobic agenda, fuelled by the continual vilification and marginalization of Islam in the media highlighted by Richardson. The EDL has been categorized as a UK phenomenon of a wider international anti-Islamic movement that arises out of the 'clash of civilizations' thesis. Alan Lake, one of the principal funders of the EDL, was concerned to steer the organization in this direction away from more traditional forms of far-right politics. The central understanding of what has become known as the 'Counter Jihad' movement is that Islam is a threat to the West and needs to be countered. Nigel Copsey has outlined Lake's agenda:

> For Lake there are four fundamental freedoms that western civilization must defend: free speech, democracy, equality in law and cultural tolerance. For Lake Islam is antithetical to all four freedoms because in his view it rejects free speech; favours theocracy over democracy; does not recognize equality in the law but Sharia law; and finally, is intolerant of other non-Islamic cultures.[16]

Chris Allen has argued that this represents an Islamophobic response to the real presence of Islam in the UK, an attempt to construct an ideology of who is included in the understanding of 'us' that excludes Muslims and Islamic identity by the misrepresentation and exaggeration of difference. This he argues correlates with Martin Barker's analysis of 'new racism' in the 1980s.[17]

Lake's presentation disturbingly correlates with characterizations of Muslims presented in some evangelical material on Islam[18] and with Nazir-Ali's comments above. It is for this reason that perhaps other Christians need to take even more seriously the criticism implicit in the report issued by the Muslim interfaith group Faith Matters in 2012 on faith responses to the EDL, particularly in relation to EDL appropriation of faith traditions for its cause:

It is interesting to note the relatively minor response from Christian communities in relation to the EDL's appropriation of their faith. The main Sikh, Jewish and Hindu organizations in the UK have released official representative statements condemning the EDL, but their Christian counterparts have remained quiet.[19]

This chapter takes this critique seriously and would want to add the importance of addressing Christian contributions to discourse on Islam such as Nazir-Ali's above, which could be seen as part of a continuum of Islamophobic discourse linking such supposedly 'respectable' utterances with the more lurid presentations of the tabloid press and the violently Islamophobic chants of the EDL demonstration. While I share the concern of Faith Matters about the lack of outspoken national leadership on this, I aim in this chapter to highlight grassroots activity by Christians in response to the EDL in cooperation with their Muslim neighbours.

The EDL has largely organized itself by way of street protests in areas with significant Muslim populations. They have often been concerned to articulate themselves in ways that are perceived differently from other traditional far-right movements. Chris Allen has explored their attempt to present themselves as a 'multicultural' movement by claiming support from the Sikh, Jewish and LGBT communities, although any involvement by such communities has been minuscule.[20] The EDL would perhaps be more correctly categorized as an Islamophobic response to the realities of multiculturalism. Gabriele Marranci has argued that Islamophobia represents a fear of the legitimate and creative possibilities inherent in a multiculturalism that includes a genuine dialogue between Islamic values and those perceived as Western.[21] The EDL's base has largely been built among the networks of football hooligan groups such as Casuals United.[22] As noted, the street protests target areas with significant Muslim populations and would be easily described, by many of the different analyses of the concept, as virulently Islamophobic. It is these street protests that have provided the concern within targeted localities. It is often felt that the EDL's aim is to incite a response from local Muslim youth, in particular on the lines of the 2001 Bradford riots; this will then incite further violence and division. It is this agenda of inciting a tide of 'cumulative extremism', correlated with a 'clash of civilizations' thesis, that lies at the heart of the EDL's agenda.[23] For local Muslim communities, it is the fear of the criminalization of Muslim youth provoked by the EDL street protests that is often of greatest concern.

Christians Responding to the EDL and Research Methodology

This section of this chapter will explore three grassroots Christian responses to EDL activity. It is based on qualitative semi-standardized interviews with individuals who played a key role in the responses in their area. I read these engagements through an interpretative lens that has been outlined in previous chapters, particularly Chapters 1 and 2: that of a practical theology of interfaith engagement. As previously outlined in this approach, theologizing about Christian interfaith engagement is firmly located in the experiences of Christian practitioners themselves. This hermeneutical model of practical theology gives primacy to the experiences of Christians engaged at a grassroots level in interfaith engagement over more systematic or fundamental approaches that privilege the application of more abstract theological and philosophical constructions. The principal questions for this methodology are: how do Christian interfaith practitioners live out their discipleship in a multifaith world; and what, theologically, is being expressed in their activity? The participants in this exploration represent active agents in Christian engagement with responses to the EDL in three English cities/towns: Bradford, Luton and Tower Hamlets in London. As well as seeking to prioritize the experience of the practitioners as the foundation for theological reflection over and above the more abstract theological methodologies, the narrative approach adopted seeks to highlight the practitioners' stories and their activity as a 'public speaking' equally relevant and perhaps more so than interviews in the *Daily Telegraph* by bishops or statements from the church hierarchies understandably sought by Faith Matters. Therefore the need to name the participants is an important part of the research, bringing into the wider debate on Christian–Muslim relations the voice of local activists on the ground. As part of this process of bringing local voices to bear on a national debate, the participants engaged agreed to their naming before interview and had the power to edit what was reported to have been said by them, though in the event no significant editing was required. As part of this research, interviews were also undertaken with activists in Leicester, but space did not permit using this material. In the event the choice of Tower Hamlets, Luton and Bradford was to present significantly different contexts with different protagonists – a radically engaged local Anglican leadership alongside a grassroots women's initiative and an evangelically inspired peace and reconciliation witness, in three areas that have come under significant media scrutiny and featured prominently in Islamophobic discourse.[24]

It is also important to reflect on my own standpoint in this research. I myself have been involved in activism in Birmingham alongside dialogue partners in the Muslim community in response to EDL incursions into the city. I come as a long-term interfaith activist who has participated in joint actions with Muslims not just in relation to the EDL but also in relation to international affairs, and community resistance to institutionalized Islamophobia in both Leeds and Birmingham. These experiences form part of what I bring to the analysis of the stories of the participants and will inevitably influence my concluding reflections. Drawing on and adapting feminist standpoint theory,[25] this research aims to be a contribution to the construction of a narrative that gives voice both to the particularities of the contexts studied but also to the wider movement of Christians engaged in similar responses that often go unreported or are marginalized in the Church's understanding of itself in relation to its Muslim neighbours. This is particularly important given the weight of a dominant Islamophobic discourse, which is often given a Christian justification or tacit support, as in the case of the former Bishop of Rochester above, and the silence of church hierarchies highlighted by Faith Matters.

'Whose Mosques? Our Mosques!': Tower Hamlets Interfaith Forum

The starting point for Fr Alan Green was the importance of understanding the long-term nature of the relationship between Christians and Muslims in Tower Hamlets and particularly his relationship, as a leading local Anglican clergy person, with Dilwar Khan, a leading figure in the East London Mosque, through the Interfaith Forum. Alan has spent 16 years ministering in the locality, with a number of years as the Area Dean of the Tower Hamlets deanery of the Church of England. He is keen to locate the whole exploration of the EDL and the local response to the targeting of Tower Hamlets within an understanding of the impact in London of the Stephen Lawrence inquiry and the subsequent exploration by police and local authorities of race hate and then the increasing engagement with the need to recognize the reality of faith hate crime, particularly Islamophobia. This shifting agenda was a challenge for local authority and police alike. The concentration on Islamophobia was a challenge to the traditional understandings of local politics that were dominated by the white left and a form of Bangladeshi communalism. The establishment of the Interfaith Forum in 2003 began the development of relations between the East London Mosque and other faith communities in the borough, particularly the local leadership of the Church of England. The arrival of Islamophobia on the local council's agenda began to create a space for an increased recognition of the role of faith generally within the public square. For Alan, the importance of this cannot be overestimated, and the dialogue that followed was instrumental in establishing strong relationships that would be drawn on at the time both of the 7/7 bombings and of the invasions of the EDL.

Although some Christians in the borough felt the emphasis on privileging Islam through the faith hate agenda was problematic, for Alan and others it was an opportunity to raise the profile of faith generally and to ensure that the Church was at the table of discussion on issues of the 'common good' and building significant relationships.

Alan explained that the interest of the EDL in Tower Hamlets was directly related to the Islamophobic discourse about the borough in the national press as 'Britain's first Islamic Republic'[26] because of the Muslim majority in the population. This was accompanied by a narrative that claimed that Christians were unwelcome in Tower Hamlets. Alan says:

> These presentations were not representative of the experience of people living on the ground in the area but combined with the writings of Andrew Gilligan[27] who has a real axe to grind about here and web sites where people just write what they want. The material for the EDL narrative was easily found. It is therefore important to realize that although there is a strong historical narrative in this area of solidarity and diversity, that story can be easily undermined and therefore it is important not to be complacent and to keep working at opposing myths that have built up in national press and elsewhere.

This was true with the first announcement of the EDL coming to Tower Hamlets in 2010. Alan states that there was a real fear in the Muslim community that 'the Christians are coming to get us'. Although at that time the EDL did not come as planned, the newly formed United East End[28] still held a rally and the importance of a visible presence of Christians through clergy on the platform helped dispel the sense that was growing, particularly among some Muslim youth, that this was a Christian–Muslim conflict playing into the EDL's 'cumulative extremism' and 'clash of civilizations' agenda. Alan and others' involvement helped to challenge that notion forcefully. Over the three years of engagement with EDL attacks on the area, increasingly the United East End interpretation and Alan's own perception was to talk about this being an attack on Tower Hamlets. He says:

> This was not just about Muslims and seeing that was really important . . . in the 2011 mobilization against the EDL the chant was 'whose streets, our streets'. By 2013 the chant had become 'whose streets, our streets; whose mosques, our

mosques' from everybody – it is about all of us; you attack the mosque, you attack my mosque.

This counters the ideological Islamophobia identified by Allen above with a clear recognition of Islam as part of the fabric of Tower Hamlets society. In a similar vein I am struck, when listening to Alan, how the agenda of the possibility of 'cumulative extremism' is articulated. He reflects on the tactic of the EDL of occasionally turning up in small numbers and doing something provocative in an attempt to garner a response from local youth:

> This is an attempt to criminalize our young people. This is a key strategy to the whole thing for us: how do we stop our young people, first, being taken in by the extremist descriptions of what is going on and second, how we stop them being criminalized?

Alan's inclusive impulse of talking of local Muslim youth as 'our young people' again counters the 'otherness' of Islam presented by Lake and other more 'respectable' Islamophobic narratives.

Alan also points out that a number of other Christians were involved, some through London Citizens (a popular community organizing network in East London), particularly Roman Catholic and more open evangelical churches; however, he identifies a difference of ecclesiology between his own and those he drew into the struggle from the Church of England and the community organizing mobilization of some church communities. In Alan's view, for Roman Catholic churches and for evangelical churches it is about signing up to something that fits clearly with the social justice agenda that is a part of Roman Catholic social teaching and increasingly core to an open evangelical church's missional theology. However, for Alan, no such consensus is possible within his own ecclesial community and neither is it about taking an agreed missional agenda into the activity in solidarity with others. Central to his own self-understanding of his activity is an Anglican incarnational theology. He says:

> The Church needs to be there . . . it needs to be there not just leading as Christians but supporting, being neighbourly most

importantly, being a part of other people's agendas as well as our own. But also . . . the Church, more importantly the Church of England, needs to regain credibility nationally and locally as a local presence, positive and open to engagement with others in solidarity and creativity. We are too taken by a nineteenth-century rhetoric about our place in the world . . . we can be too easily dismissed by secular bodies and groups who assume we always have a 'Christian' agenda.

By being willing to enter the mess and confusion of community relationships and not concerned with being seen to be engaged with the 'wrong people', the Church mirrors the relationships it seeks to encourage within itself as a broad Church engaging with difference between those who participate within it. Alan argues that the Church should have an agenda that seeks, in the activity of solidarity with Muslims as part of a wider community response, to discover God in our neighbours. In the openness and willingness to support, encourage and join in wider agendas (such as resisting Islamophobia), the Church can rediscover itself and be discovered by others, as partners for the common good. Alan recounts the story of speaking with Dilwar Khan, at a large Muslim event on interfaith and community working. A question was posed from someone who was from a different part of London, concerned that she could get no one in her moribund Interfaith Forum really interested in engaging in more practical activity. Dilwar responded to this by saying: 'Go and find out who your local Church of England clergy are and go and talk to them, because they will understand, talk through the issues and they will engage with you.'

Alan talks of a conscious strategy of bringing the Church into discussions in the borough through joining the important agenda of addressing Islamophobia and other needs perceived to be issues facing the Muslim community. In his view, the Church must actively seek a place at the table and prove itself worthy of being there rather than getting resentful when it is not invited, or overly concerned about being associated with groups that do not share a similar ethos. This was particularly true for Alan in the relationship that he and Dilwar Khan built up with Unite Against

Fascism (UAF). Other church responses have sought to distance themselves from the UAF but the strength of the relationship between mosque and church in Tower Hamlets and the central role of the Interfaith Forum meant that the UAF worked with the faith communities' agenda. Alan was also conscious of needing to affirm a plurality of responses to the EDL, from prayers and vigils in churches to joining in demonstrations. There were many ways one could respond, but the Church *had* to respond – it could not avoid expressing solidarity with Muslim neighbours and resistance to the EDL's agenda of 'saving' Christians in Tower Hamlets. This was the focus of the EDL's 2013 mobilization, fuelled by scurrilous material in some national newspapers. The Church was being presented as dead or dying and as an elderly unwanted presence in the East End that was being 'taken over' by Muslims. Alan says:

> Our response was to say 'No you are not saving the Church or rescuing us; the Church is a part of this community and we are alive and present in this area.' One paper showed false pictures of small congregations alongside packed mosques, which were fabricated pictures. But the point was that this is not how we live and this is not how we decide if the Church is successful or not . . . our ministry is to be at the heart of the community continuing to worship within this place and continuing to support and be engaged with everyone who lives around you because we are part of it and the Church only understands itself in relation to the wider community and the Church only knows God by worshipping God in church and meeting God in our neighbour.

'The Ribbons Were a Sacrament': Bradford Women for Peace

Liz Firth and Clare MacLaren were involved in a women's response to the EDL invasion of Bradford in 2010, while Liz also reflected on a later visit in 2013. Clare was new to the area in 2010, as a recently appointed Anglican vicar, while Liz, a Roman

Catholic, was 'Bradford born and bred', had been involved in community work in the city for a number of years and at the time was a local Church Action on Poverty community worker. At the time of interview she worked for Bradford's Anglican cathedral as their interfaith worker.

Liz locates the women's response to the EDL firmly within the story of the 2001 riots provoked by the far-right groups the British National Party and National Front demonstrating in the city.[29] For her, and other Christian women who worked closely with Muslim women in community work, the aim was to address women's concerns that the same thing should not happen as in 2001, when young men from Bradford's Asian community ended up receiving hefty prison sentences following the riots. The women felt that they were 'hoodwinked' in 2001, unaware that there was the possibility of trouble, and wanted to ensure this did not happen again. Initially the aim was to ensure that women were involved and informed during the process of preparation for the EDL demonstration, and Liz and others sought to ensure good channels of communication existed between the authorities and Muslim women, particularly on the ground. But circumstances changed and the women's meetings began to explore the need to respond differently to the EDL compared to other initiatives that were developing.

Unlike Tower Hamlets, the structures and depth of relationship between faith leaders did not exist at the time in Bradford, and the organizing networks of the faith communities were relatively weak. This allowed the UAF to impose its own template on attempts to organize a response that emphasized a strongly confrontational approach to the EDL. Meanwhile the national network, Hope not Hate, began working with the local media to call on the Home Secretary to ban the EDL march. While this heightened awareness of the issue, it was not going to stop a static protest and an EDL presence in the city on the day. The women's response, which became Bradford Women for Peace (BWFP), took a different approach: they sought to prevent the EDL from setting the agenda. The group included Christians, Muslims and women from other faiths and no faith. Liz reflects on how easy it was to get Christian women involved: 'They absolutely didn't need persuading. Clare as a vicar, Methodist ministers, Catholic lay activists and women religious all got involved, more so than the church leadership.' For Clare, the motivation was obvious:

> As Christians we needed to stand in solidarity with our Muslim brothers and sisters in this city and to say that those in the EDL who would claim to be flying the banner of Christianity do not do so in our name or in the name of any legitimate understanding of our faith.

Clare remembers the idea that became the response, being part of a 'coalescence of creative thinking': after much debate it was decided that they were not going to be present during the day, in order to avoid a confrontational approach. The discussion moved in the direction of asking: 'If we can't be there, what can we leave as a footprint to show that we have been there?' From this question the idea emerged of going into the city centre the day before and covering it with green ribbons. Liz remembers that the green was both a 'nod to Islam' but also wrapped up in a symbolism of growth and creativity. Clare thinks the Day-Glo nature of the green was to ensure it wasn't seen too much as a 'Muslim thing'. The women went into the city centre on the Friday afternoon for two to three hours, giving out ribbons to wear and covering major city-centre sites with green fabric. Although Liz and local Muslim activist Wahida Shaffi were the spokeswomen for the group, the group was immensely diverse and had drawn in women from refugee communities, Muslim and Christian, who saw the EDL as representing something they had fled; Christian and Muslim women raised or long-term residents in Bradford; old-style peace campaigners; and young women new to any kind of activism. But there were significant gaps in the representation of women in the city, something that Liz was particularly aware of in her reflections, although in some ways the absence – for instance of white working-class women from estates in the city – was addressed on the day when the diverse group that made up BWFP entered the city, gave out ribbons and listened to people's stories, often from those women who were missing from the group. This whole experience spoke to Liz of the lack of women's voice across the board in all communities, and it was from this observation that an initiative arose: Giving Women Voice in Bradford. This initiative, while being successful in raising up women's voices from the Pakistani heritage Muslim community, has not been able to make inroads into engaging and empowering women from the white working class, despite attempts.

Clare reflected on the theological implications of the ribbons as a 'real absence', a statement that women were not present because of men's violence. She says:

> the ribbons were our resistance, they were a real absence in a theological sense, a form of sacrament, an outward and visible sign of an inward reality, that reality was the possibility of peace and hope for Bradford despite the negative presence of the EDL and the importance of women's involvement in public life. We are here, our footprint is all over the city centre. This is a spiritual energy and vibrancy that will not be overcome, an act of resistance that will catch your eye whether you like it or not – a challenge and a comfort.

The centrality of gender in the whole issue was starkly present in the gathering on Friday evening, organized through Hope not Hate and billed as an interfaith event. Not one woman was on the platform. Both Clare and Liz expressed their anger at this: 'they gave us a clap', says Liz sarcastically. The significance of the lack of involvement of women was unappreciated by the organizers, who saw that they had persuaded all the 'right people' to be there: civic and religious leaders. For Clare:

> This represented something that is wrong about our religious institutions, both Muslim and Christian, in a sense that women don't have a voice on the public stage . . . this symbolized for me two contrasting ways of interfaith working in the city. First, the hierarchical representative model, where a man from the church meets a man from the mosque, or the diocese and the council of mosques, and a representative meeting is said to have taken place; though in what way it has filtered down into

the communities they are supposed to be representing is questionable. And then, second, there is the on-the-ground stuff with women and men working together getting on with the day-to-day stuff in their communities.

Clare cites the interfaith nature of the governing body of the local primary school of which she is chair, as an example of the grassroots work, which is also about consciously listening to each other and constructing visions for what they want for their children: a bigger vision than faith meeting faiths; instead people of faith, working together with others, for a greater whole. She describes the relationship with her Muslim woman vice-chair and how, when they engaged in conversation on a difficult issue in the school, they shared insights from their traditions and engaged in a dialogue that includes their mutual exploration of God. For Clare, so much of official interfaith working in Bradford maintains a stance of wanting to assert the superiority of one's own tradition however consciously or unconsciously this is done. Alternatively, her experience of generating within herself and seeing in her partners an 'appreciative inquiry' into the other is something that she feels needs to be explored more widely. She distinguishes the 'devout and affiliated' from the 'devout and unaffiliated', as a difference between those who identify strongly with the institutional forms of their tradition and those who still practise and have a deep relationship with the tradition but sit more lightly to the institutions. She finds this latter mode the most creative and the one she engages in most fully with Muslim women in her community, often leading to an openness that she describes as a 'universal embrace'. The contrasting image of women's interfaith leadership in Clare's local primary school and the patriarchal model presented at the 2010 vigil represents for her the two modes of interfaith engagement.

Alternatively, Liz reflects on the impact of the women's action in 2010 on that first 'official' hierarchical interfaith model, which she sees as having improved, although not in terms of gender representation. When the EDL came again in 2013 it was easy to get faith leaders involved; when the bombing of churches took place in Pakistan it was the Council of Mosques that issued a statement condemning the attacks and inviting representatives of the churches to a meeting to express their solidarity and concern; a significant development but again not involving women. She, as a lay community worker, was the only woman invited. At the time of interview, the visit of 'Britain First'[30] to the city and its mosques led to strongly worded condemnations from Christian ecumenical bodies and the Anglican Church. For Liz, this improved interfaith communication is to be applauded and is a direct result of the 2010 response in the city to the EDL and Christian involvement in that. But it also raises other questions that take her back to her concern for the involvement of white working-class women. She reflects on how, for Christians, it is increasingly notable that faith is a permissible agenda and, as in Tower Hamlets, Islam has created a space for faith in public life. However, she wonders if there is a need to recognize that a significant part of the community do not and will not identify with faith and that the role of the Church in this case, rather than seeing them as the 'unchurched' needing conversion, is to create space for a consciously secular agenda as a valid contribution to dialogue concerning civic life. Liz asks if there is a need for the Church to reflect on how it can broker what is perhaps more of an intercultural rather than interfaith process in the city. How can it express a genuine interest in these communities' concerns and enable their voice to be heard and them to hear others' as Bradford moves forward?

'Live at Peace with All' – Witnessing to Christ's Peace in Luton

Peter Adams speaks of the work in Luton as rooted in his own peace and reconciliation background. Peter came to Luton with a background in Christian youth work, with Youth with a Mission and work in intercultural conflict resolution. He located his independent work at St Mary's in Luton's town centre; although Peter is a freelance consultant and teacher, the church welcomed his basing his work there and has financially supported some of his projects. He works internationally and nationally on peace and conflict resolution but his local presence and involvement has also been significant, particularly in relation to engaging the EDL. After moving to Luton, Peter became involved in 'cohesion' work in the town and was also involved in the very active Luton Council of Faiths. This background was important to the response to the EDL; for instance, for two years he was involved with an interfaith group in putting on Holocaust Memorial Day. He reflects:

> We always treated the preparation for HMD as an engagement in and of itself; it was an encounter as we processed the material as a multifaith group and made it live for us. In 2009, just as we were preparing for it, the Israelis went into Gaza and the Muslims who had been involved fully before then said, 'We are not getting involved'. We said 'NO!' and through negotiations and dialogue we ended up with an event that included Christians, Muslims and Jews saying, 'Whatever happens elsewhere in the world we are for peace in our town.'

Peter reflects that this was a significant piece of groundwork for what lay ahead in responding to the EDL.

Soon after this, the 2nd East Anglian regiment, which included soldiers from Luton, had a homecoming parade on 10 March 2009 after a tour of duty in Iraq. This was a large lunchtime gathering to welcome home the troops. A small group of 14 or so Al-Muhajiroun[31] activists sought to disrupt the event, leading to an angry response from others gathered, and a riot involving around 250 people ensued. It became clear with hindsight that this was perhaps a classic example of 'cumulative extremism', mentioned above, as later research showed that far-right elements had been involved in the crowd, were expecting Al-Muhajiroun intervention on the day and wanted to use this to initiate the trouble. Things became even more heightened in the town as, a few weeks later, in early May 2009, there was the firebombing of the mosque. Peter reflects:

> We as a Council of Faiths survive in a town that does so easily get trouble by building bridges across troubled waters.

Something happens; we are round the next day and engage. In a smallish town you can do something significant. The local vicar, the Convenor of the Council of Faiths and myself went around to the mosque in the morning expressing our solidarity.

He also reflects on how his own conflict resolution background brought a different dynamic to the council of faiths:

I sometimes saw interfaith work as really good at positive engagement but not so good at the difficulties, whether that is conflict or doctrinal difference, but we couldn't brush over this. I was coming from a conflict-resolution background; I took conflict by the hand. We needed a press conference and to oppose what happened. Already a narrative of protecting Christian religion was around; the BNP were at a high point with the European elections of 2009 and their campaign with the rhetoric of 'saving Christianity' already strongly present. The Christians in the town needed to speak. So we got the Churches Together group into doing a press statement. The draft took a week to agree. I went to all the denominational leaders in the town and they were cautious, as were the Council of Mosques. This was going beyond where most people were willing to go or had been in the past, but eventually people went for it. We organized a press conference and the BBC and ITV were present.

Peter felt that this was a significant response, which laid the foundations for the next five years of working for peace in a town that was home to both the EDL leadership and a small but vocal group of Al-Muhajiroun activists.

The Press conference and statement were vitally important. We put a stake in the road that said we are not prepared to allow the extremists to divide us in the town. We are going to hold the centre, as Christian and Muslim leaders, and work to deal with our own extremists. It was a statement of faith but I think we got through the next five years because we did what we did then.

In drafting the statement Peter and others were influenced by both the *A Common Word Between Us* statement of Muslim scholars worldwide[32] and the Yale Divinity School's[33] response to this, headed up by the theologian Miroslav Volf and his work on Muslim–Christian relations. The statement in full is as follows:

> In recent weeks Luton has again been seen in the media as a place of Islamic extremism and nationalist extremism. Yet the reality is that these small extremist groups do not represent the majority of the community.
>
> As Muslims and Christians in Luton we are committed to grow in understanding of each other and to work together for good. In doing so we are inspired and challenged by words that lie at the heart of each of our Holy Scriptures, where we are commanded to love God and love our neighbour. As neighbours in this town, we need to discover the things that unite us, and celebrate those. Where we are different we are committed to seek understanding and trust, rather than resorting to hatred and strife. Let us respect each other, be fair, just and kind to one another and live in sincere peace, harmony and mutual goodwill.
>
> In this time of tension we are calling for people of all communities and every area of life in Luton to take every opportunity to strengthen our unity. Many of us work or study together, some of us are neighbours, but fewer socialize and far fewer have deep friendships. Let's use every opportunity we have to build up the common ground between us.
>
> To indicate your support by signing the commitment, to read latest news, to see what people are doing to work for peace and unity, and to tell us your own plans: AND spread the word!
>
> Most importantly, invite your Muslim or Christian colleagues, neighbours or friends to join you!

Two weeks later, United People of Luton, organized by the nucleus that became the EDL, had a demonstration that led to serious disturbances in the town and at one point it looked as though they might break into the main Muslim area in the town,

Bury Park. The difference between the Luton context and the other two case studies is highlighted here. In Luton there was an element of cumulative extremism that fed the local dynamic: as has been said, a small Al-Muhajiroun group had been active in the town for a while, and although it took a while to fully realize it, Luton became the base for the EDL. However, even before that was realized it is important to note the local character of these early non-, or embryonic EDL demonstrations. Elsewhere the response to the EDL was based on a sense of invasion, and local mobilization to respond to this was seen as defending the local community against outside extremism. In Luton, with both the presence of Al-Muhajiroun and a local base for EDL, there was quite a different dynamic. This was reflected in the attitude of the church towards the local United People of Luton movement (early name of local EDL). Peter refers to this as a pastoral approach, challenging but pastoral:

> We identified a number of people who had been in youth groups or were still in relationships with youth leaders, perhaps watched the football together, people with parents in churches, people with neighbours in churches and we quickly picked up a network of several people we tried to keep contact with. As a result we tried to approach it pastorally. In summary we believe the heart of our work around the EDL has been an appropriate interpretation of the 'cure of souls' for all in our parishes. Early on we discovered EDL support included the sons and daughters of church members, former or current youth group members, friends of friends, neighbours. We used some of those channels to reach out to leaders, and over the years have had considerable engagement with EDL leaders. With this in mind, that these were our parishioners rather than our enemies, we tried to use the language of pastoral care rather than the language of 'Fight the fascists!' At the same time we sought to be good and caring neighbours for our Muslim community.

This led to conflict with the UAF; the traditional left-wing anti-fascist approach did not fit well with the quite distinctive peace and reconciliation agenda that both the Christians and

Muslim leadership in the town were beginning to embrace, and as in Bradford, the UAF and local Christians largely worked in quite different directions. This was reflected when what had become the EDL announced that they were organizing a demonstration in the town at the end of the summer of 2009. By this time significant demonstrations had happened elsewhere, including Birmingham. Peter tells the story:

> The EDL didn't show on the first date of 30 August, although UAF mobilized; however, a text announcing that the EDL were invading Bury Park circulated and within minutes 250 Muslim lads lined up with bricks and a conflict with the police ensued, with the result that 30 Muslim lads ended up with prison sentences.

Luton had experienced in a smaller way what Bradford had done years before with the events of 2001.

For Peter, the anger and hatred he felt present at UAF meetings disturbed both him and the local Muslim leaders who were involved in the events around the statement. Another demonstration was planned for a month later. The focus became, as it had been elsewhere in both Bradford and Tower Hamlets, avoiding confrontation between the police and Muslim youth. The cat and mouse tactics of the EDL at this time reflected their attempt to provoke local disturbances between police and Muslim youth, as was shown in the Tower Hamlets case. In such circumstances the priority was to work to avoid such confrontation and in doing so to blunt the tactics of the EDL. Peter takes up the story again:

> We worked fervently for the next three weeks as they were due to come at the end of September. Again, they didn't come, but we worked with police about not having a high presence, allowing the community to steward with the police in background; Christian leaders with Muslims and community workers were out working the area and we succeeded. That was a game changer, that we could work with community and do something significant; the police were deeply positive that day about our ability to have an impact on events.

The next significant event was the coming out of 'Tommy Robinson' and the clear connection of the EDL leadership with Luton established in Autumn 2010. The EDL then announced what they called a 'homecoming' – in February 2011 they said they were going to bring 12,000–20,000; in fact it was 5,000–8,000 on the day. A lot of preparation work was done and Peter and a Muslim partner went to every meeting of the police planning group. The wider Christian community was heavily involved, with Street Pastors, City Centre Chaplaincy all seriously engaged, along with ecumenical leaders. Peter reflects on the building of a community mediation structure for the day – groups including a Muslim, a Christian, a police officer and a youth worker were sent out together to be on the ground in the town. These mediation groups were under police control but the church and Muslim community groups also had people in both EDL and UAF demonstrations. St Mary's in the town centre acted as a place of refuge. As in 2009, the police presence was low key in Bury Park, the heart of the Muslim area – though in the rest of town there were nearly 2,000 police. Again there were clashes in tactics with the UAF, who although located in their counter-demonstration away from EDL and Bury Park, still managed to get some rogue groups into Bury Park and, at a time when the EDL were actually leaving Luton, were circulating information that the EDL was about to break into Bury Park. Again it was local Muslim community activists who managed to stop a repeat of the 30 August 2009 trouble: with 100 Muslim stewards out in Bury Park with a small number of Christian ministers, the message in 2011 was that the UAF was not to be supported within the Muslim community. The following year, with a return of the EDL, the Muslim community became more involved with their counter-demonstration after the UAF had spent a year rooting themselves more locally and building connections in Bury Park. This led to a different approach between Christian and Muslim community activists, although they continued to liaise and work together. However, it was not only UAF tactics with which Peter's peace and reconciliation approach came into conflict. The EDL wanted to march from Farley Estate in 2011, which they regarded as their 'heartland', and march into town. Peter argued with the police about this. He saw this as an attempt to develop a 'Belfast mentality' in Luton; as directly related to Alan Lake's understanding, mentioned earlier, of wanting to develop a sectarian division in cities between 'white' and 'multicultural' areas. The police argued that it was their human right to march in such a way but Peter was consistent in his challenge, and that and a change of circumstances led to the plan being denied. Peter reflects: 'We worked with people as Christians but also challenged them – police, town hall, Muslim community.'

Peter describes the work as Christian peacemaking and says he is inspired by such groups as Peace Catalyst International in his approach. He comes from a theologically conservative tradition rooted in an evangelical charismatic background and sees this work as missional. There is a real sense, in his description of his work, that Peter is involved in witnessing to Christ via the reconciliation work, building respect within the Muslim community, including being invited to Muslim groups to speak about Jesus and being identified and congratulated by Muslims for his work when walking around the town. He also reflects on how his work has had an impact on St Mary's and its developing interpretation of the gospel as rooted in an understanding of peace. The church has on its doors the inscription 'Live at peace with all', which can be read on the way into and out of the church. For Peter this is central to understanding both how the Christian community should live together as they gather for the Eucharist, the act of sharing the Peace being an important part of that acknowledgement of approaching the table for the sacrament in a state of peace with fellow Christians, but also the call to go out and 'Live at peace with all' in the town. He remembers how at a Vigil held at the church before one of the EDL demonstrations, his word was rooted in the church's inscription. Christians, he reflected, are called to live at peace with all, and the EDL, which claims Christian heritage, works against that gospel call.

Conclusion: Towards a Theological Engagement with Multiculturalism

It is clear from the three case studies above that grassroots Christian responses to the EDL have been significant, despite the correct identification by Faith Matters of a silence on the part of national church leadership. Christians in these areas have played important and significant roles in blunting the discourse of Islamophobia fuelled by the press and taken to the streets by the EDL. However, what in many ways is equally important in our case studies are the deeper issues for Christian–Muslim encounter and interfaith engagement that arise out of the stories.

First, secularism – a third factor in Christian–Muslim encounter – is present, particularly in the Bradford and Tower Hamlets contexts. In Tower Hamlets the negotiation between secular authorities, an increased profile and concern with Islam in civic life, and the need for the church to find its place was at the root of the local Church of England's engagement with the Interfaith Forum. In Bradford, Christians involved in a broad alliance of women, led by Christians and Muslims but involving those of no faith, articulated an awareness of the need for greater inclusiveness and a concern to avoid, through improved Christian–Muslim relations, a faith huddle. In both contexts, a public theological approach is being adopted that:

> is not primarily and directly evangelical theology which addresses the gospel to the world in hope of repentance and conversion. Rather, it is theology which seeks the welfare of the city before protecting the interests of the church.[34]

Certainly, our activists display in their public theological sensitivities a very different agenda from that displayed by Nazir-Ali[35] in his recent book that sets secularism, Islam, and multiculturalism as a 'triple jeopardy' for contemporary society.

Second, the story of Bradford points to the importance of feminist and practical theological critique of interfaith encounter and theology of religions. Clare MacLaren's analysis, both of gender dynamics and of the two types of interfaith engagement, bring feminist and practical theological insights into the field, which is refreshing in its critique of *both* Christian and Islamic patriarchal practices and the overcoming of these hierarchies in grassroots work, which prioritizes a mutually enriching sharing of spirituality in action over the debating of difference. Equally, the abiding impact of the women's initiative on interfaith relations in the city cannot go unnoticed, nor can the continued activity of this movement in Bradford as it gathers a cosmopolitan mix of women to take the lead on global issues having a local impact that brings together concern for women-only led activity from Islamic and feminist perspectives in conversation.

In Luton an approach founded on a significant international dialogical document from the Muslim community, *A Common Word Between Us*, and substantial Christian responses to that led to a consciously peace and reconciliation approach in a town where the dynamics of 'cumulative extremism' were more locally developed and apparent. The reality of significant EDL involvement locally also saw an approach that brought, alongside a concern to be good neighbours to local Muslim citizens, a concern to reach out to those influenced by the EDL in a pastoral approach that sought to get 'under their skin', to understand and to challenge. Although similar to the Bradford and Tower Hamlets contexts of working with Muslim neighbours for the common good, a more particularist influenced dialogical theology seemed to be present that saw Christ's call to peace as an important witness to the context; although not an overt 'evangelical' theology, it displayed less of the public theological concerns perhaps emphasized in the Tower Hamlets and Bradford contexts. In Tower Hamlets an incarnational approach was shown by Alan Green, where overtly consciously Christian agendas were not felt to be needed in an approach that saw the Church standing in simple solidarity with Muslim neighbours and working in a broad alliance with groups including the UAF. In Bradford the Christian Feminist approach of Clare MacLaren saw dialogue as leading to a broader expression of a resistance spirituality that she articulated in Christian terms as sacramental.

In the Bradford and Tower Hamlets contexts our interviewees' approaches meant that the practical theological hermeneutic applied to Christian–Muslim encounter draws us into a different exploration from the more dominant systematic engagements that may concentrate on the status of the Qur'an, the prophethood of Muhammad or questions of Christology. With a practical theological emphasis and an examination of Christian praxis in response to a significant manifestation of Islamophobia, we have found ourselves exploring areas of public theology that place the Church's concern for wider society at the centre, alongside the development of a non-defensive 'appreciative inquiry' into each other's spiritual resources as a strategy for building confidence to act courageously together. In Luton, although not expressed in such a public theological frame, a Christologically focused dialogue with Muslims, rooted in developing a call to represent the common good, also sees a movement away from theological contestation towards an agenda rooted in the contribution of Christians to the good of all in the town, which includes a subtle and uncoercive witness to the particularity of Christ's peace. These intimations of hopeful cooperation perhaps call us to step up to the task of developing a variety of theological discourses that challenge the narratives of fear and exclusion by embracing multiculturalism in all its complexity and problems as a potentially positive reality for human flourishing.

Notes

1 Ray Gaston, *A Heart Broken Open: Radical Faith in an Age of Fear* (Glasgow: Wild Goose Publications, 2009), pp. 16–22.

2 Robert Lambert and Jonathan Githens-Mazer, *Islamophobia and Anti-Muslim Hate Crime: UK Case Studies 2010* (Exeter: European Muslim Research Centre, 2011), pp. 20–1.

3 Michael Nazir-Ali, 'Bishop Warns of No-Go areas for Non-Muslims', interview with Jonathan Wynne-Jones in *The Telegraph*, 6 January 2008 – www.telegraph.co.uk/news/uknews/1574694/Bishop-warns-of-no-go-zones-for-non-Muslims.html (accessed 6/10/14).

4 Erick Bleich and Maxwell Rahsaan, 'Assessing Islamophobia in Britain: Where Do Muslims Really Stand?', in Marc Helbling (ed.),

Islamophobia in the West: Measuring and Explaining Individual Attitudes (London: Routledge, 2012), p. 53.

5 Clive D. Field, 'Revisiting Islamophobia in Contemporary Britain, 2007–2010', in Helbling (ed.), *Islamophobia in the West*, pp. 158–9.

6 The Commission on British Muslims and Islamophobia, *Islamophobia: A Challenge for Us All* (London: Runnymede Trust, 1997), p. 4.

7 Fred Halliday, '"Islamophobia" Reconsidered', *Ethnic and Racial Studies* 22:5 (1999), pp. 892–902.

8 Brian Klug, 'Islamophobia: A Concept Comes of Age', *Ethnicities* 12:5 (2012), pp. 665–81.

9 Tahir Abbas, 'Islamophobia in the United Kingdom: Historical and Contemporary Political and Media Discourses in the Framing of 21st-Century Anti-Muslim Racism', in John L. Esposito and Ibrahim Kalin (eds), *Islamophobia: The Challenge of Pluralism in the 21st Century* (Oxford: Oxford University Press, 2011), p. 74.

10 Nigel Copsey, Janet Dack, Mark Littler and Matthew Feldman, *Anti-Muslim Hate Crime and the Far-Right* (Centre for Fascist, Anti-Fascist and Post-Fascist Studies, Teesside University, 2013); Chris Allen, Arshad Isakjee and Öslem Ögtem Young, *Maybe We Are Hated: The Experience and Impact of Anti-Muslim Hate on British Muslim Women* (Institute of Applied Social Studies, University of Birmingham, 2013).

11 Nigel Copsey, *The English Defence League: Challenging Our Country and Our Values of Social Inclusion, Fairness and Equality* (London: Faith Matters, 2010), pp. 8–11.

12 Roger Eatwell, 'Community Cohesion and Cumulative Extremism in Contemporary Britain', *The Political Quarterly* 77:2 (April–June 2006), pp. 204–16.

13 Bernard Lewis, 'The Roots of Muslim Rage', *Atlantic Monthly* (September 1990) – www.theatlantic.com/magazine/archive/1990/09/the-roots-of-muslim-rage/304643 (accessed 6/10/14); Samuel Huntington, 'The Clash of Civilizations?', *Foreign Affairs* 72:3 (1993), pp. 22–49.

14 John E. Richardson, '"Get Shot of the Lot of Them": Election Reporting of Muslims in British Newspapers', *Patterns of Prejudice* 43:3–4 (2009), pp. 355–77.

15 Richardson, '"Get Shot of the Lot of Them"', pp. 336–7.

16 Copsey, *English Defence League*, p. 16.

17 Chris Allen, 'Opposing Islamification or Promoting Islamophobia? Understanding the English Defence League', *Pattern of Prejudice* 45:4 (2011), pp. 279–94 (p. 291).

18 Patrick Sookhdeo, *Islam in Our Midst: The Challenge to Our Christian Heritage* (McLean, VA: Issac Publishing, 2011).

19 H. S. Lane, *A Study of the English Defence League: What Draws People of Faith to Right-Wing Organisations and What Effects Does the*

EDL Have on Community Cohesion and Interfaith Relations? (London: Faith Matters, 2012), p. 16.

20 Allen, 'Opposing Islamification', p. 290.

21 Gabriele Marranci, 'Multiculturalism, Islam and the Clash of Civilizations Theory: Rethinking Islamophobia', Culture and Religion 5:1 (2004), pp. 105–17.

22 Copsey, English Defence League.

23 Matthew Feldman, From Radical-Right Islamophobia to 'Cumulative Extremism': A Paper on the Shifting Focus of Hatred (London: Faith Matters, 2012).

24 The primary research material herein is from four recorded interviews conducted by the author with the following people: Peter Adams (19 June 2014); Liz Firth (14 May 2014); Alan Green (9 May 2014); Clare MacLaren (14 May 2014). I mention the names of each participant as I cite them in the following text and so they are not referenced further.

25 Sandra Harding (ed.), The Feminist Standpoint Theory Reader: Intellectual and Political Controversies (New York: Routledge, 2004).

26 Andrew Gilligan, 'Labour: London Borough Becomes "Islamic Republic"', Daily Telegraph, 22 October 2010 – http://blogs.telegraph.co.uk/news/andrewgilligan/100060304/labour-london-borough-becomes-Islamic-republic.

27 Andrew Gilligan is a well-known British journalist. At the time referred to by Alan Green he was writing and blogging on Tower Hamlets regularly.

28 A coalition of community groups, activists and trade unions.

29 Paul Bagguley and Yasmin Hussain (eds), Riotous Citizens: Ethnic Conflict in Multicultural Britain (Aldershot: Ashgate, 2008).

30 A group coming out of the EDL that began in the Spring of 2014 aggressively visiting mosques during prayer times and handing out army-issue Bibles in an attempt to provoke reaction – see for instance www.theguardian.com/world/2014/may/13/police-far-right-invasions-bradford-glasgow-mosques-britain-first.

31 For a summary of Al-Muhajiroun's perspective, see www.hopenothate.org.uk/hate-groups/am.

32 See www.acommonword.com.

33 See www.acommonword.com/loving-god-and-neighbor-together-a-christian-response-to-a-common-word-between-us-and-you.

34 Duncan Forrester, 'The Scope of Public Theology', Studies in Christian Ethics 17:2 (2004), pp. 5–19 (p. 6).

35 Michael Nazir-Ali, Triple Jeopardy for the West: Aggressive Secularism, Radical Islam and Multiculturalism (London: Bloomsbury, 2012).

5

Rejoicing in the Truth

A Practical Theological Affirmation of Multiculturalism

Introduction

In Chapter 4, I looked at three responses to Islamophobia and in my conclusion argued that it was time to work towards theological reflection that might enable positive Christian engagement with the phenomenon of multiculturalism. Multiculturalism has certainly not had a good press in recent years. However, what often passes for a critique of multiculturalism is a parody of the reality in terms of policy practice, theoretical analysis and political vision. After exploring sympathetic understandings of multiculturalism and what Nasar Meer has positively identified as the growing 'Muslim consciousness', we will move on to explore how the dynamics of multiculturalism were manifested in the three case studies explored in the previous chapter and how each in its own way demonstrated a positive Christian engagement with multiculturalism and a developing Muslim consciousness. We will then go on to unpack in more detail how Islamophobia can be viewed as a resistance to multiculturalism as presented in Gabriele Marranci's analysis of Europe's perception of Islam as a 'transruptive' force and how this might relate both to our analysis of transmodernity in Chapter 2 and our own critique of 'Christendom' and a need for a 'disavowal of Constantine' outlined in Chapter 3. We will then explore how theology might draw on both biblical and Qur'anic sources to enable theological reflection that affirms our multicultural context and promotes it as a positive and divinely given reality. Finally, through stories of encounter between Christians and Muslims we will look at resources in both the biblical and Islamic traditions that may enable a practical theological response to Islamophobia that seeks to demonstrate how embracing multiculturalism can enable a deeper engagement with Christian values for the individual disciple in her encounter in the everyday realities of living with others in God's world.

Understanding Multiculturalism

Multiculturalism has become a bit of a dirty word in public discourse.[1] Often criticized for leading to 'segregation' and a failure of communities in 'integrate', it is argued that it has naively been a contributing factor to the supposed rise of 'Islamic extremism' and a failure in enabling predominantly Muslim communities to integrate into society in the UK. This public discourse, which has advocates on both the mainstream political left and right, has academic and social policy backing from the growing engagement with interculturalism[2] as a potential replacement for multiculturalism as both a policy framework and a philosophy for understanding the increasingly diverse nature of European society. The argument in its most liberal form claims that multiculturalism encouraged an essentialism of group identities that restricted people's ability to integrate into wider society and often also failed to address inequalities within the groups whose 'difference' was affirmed and encouraged through funding opportunities for cultural development. The argument that a conscious multiculturalism has informed British social policy for decades has been seriously questioned by people such as the sociologist Tariq Modood.[3] Modood argues that little in the way of conscious multicultural policies has been enacted by central government. Modood is clear in his defence of multiculturalism that the problem is not that too much multiculturalism has informed public policy but that a conscious and overt multiculturalism has failed to be articulated in mainstream national political discourse. However, it would be true to say that multiculturalism has significantly informed local developments, particularly in educational authorities and municipal government. As Gurharpal Singh has argued:

> Historically, multiculturalism as a public policy in Britain, has been heavily localized, often made voluntary, and linked essentially to issues of managing diversity in areas of immigrant settlement. The legislative framework on which this policy is based . . . recognized this contingency, giving additional resources to local authorities as well as new powers to promote racial and ethnic equality. With these enabling powers, most local authorities with large ethnic minority populations have transformed themselves from initially being the bastions of official racism to being promoters of anti-racism and multiculturalism, and with this change the strength of local ethnic communities and coalitions have been instrumental.[4]

Often, critique of multiculturalism is based on a misunderstanding of its meaning; others see more sinister forces at work in the critique, where rejecting multiculturalism is central to 'laundering increasingly acceptable forms of racism'.[5] As Ali Rattansi has pointed out:

> Multiculturalism has never been about encouraging separation and segregation. It has involved the creation of structures in which the incorporation of immigrants and ethnic minorities occurs fairly and with the recognition that the desire of immigrants and minorities to retain aspects of their cultures is reasonable, and that cultural diversity is itself desirable and benefits the nation in a variety of ways.[6]

Modood has argued that multiculturalism sits alongside other views of 'integration' or how 'difference' can be unproblematized in European societies' experience in the postwar period of increased migration from former imperial colonies and beyond. He cites four alternative approaches to engaging with difference.[7]

First, assimilation – a one-way process in which newcomers 'do little to disturb the society they are settling in and become as much like their new compatriots as possible'. Modood argues that while assimilation as a term has been largely dropped in public discourse on immigration and race relations in the UK from the 1960s, contemporary discussions on integration often include a high degree of an assimilationist agenda, particularly in contemporary political discourse on Islam, Muslim communities and British identity. This requires a thorough critical inspection of arguments for integration, particularly those critical of multiculturalism. Two forms of 'non-assimilative integration – a two-way process where members of the majority community as well as immigrants and ethnic minorities are required to do something' – are also in operation, one that he terms individualist integration, where minority cultures have individual rights to expression in the private realm but are not overly acknowledged in their difference or funded to encourage expression in the public sphere; and second, multiculturalism that sees integration as both two-way and involving both individuals and groups. He argues that multiculturalism more clearly seeks to address areas of prejudice, discrimination and exclusion in the integration process and presents more of a challenge to the dominant culture to engage in a two-way process of integration embracing different cultures as an integral part of a new understanding of the wider society. Finally, the fourth category, cosmopolitanism, asserts the reality of diversity but seeks to deconstruct group identities both of supposed minorities and of the dominant culture. Celebrating diversity, experimentation and cultural exploration, cosmopolitanism encourages people to view themselves as 'global citizens' able to sample from the diversity on offer and construct fluid identities rather than encourage what are seen as fixed and potentially oppressive religious, ethnic or national identities. Cosmopolitanism can be challenged about its potential to develop a deconstruction and potentially oppressive relativizing of solidarity-orientated group identities in its race to celebrate the complexities of diversity.

The urban theologian Chris Shannahan has argued that multiculturalism has become a 'zombie category' that requires a 'hermeneutics of liberative difference' to breathe new life into it. He presents the current dominant narrative against multiculturalism as arguing in favour of assimilation to a reductionist view of 'Britishness' informed consciously or unconsciously by the 'clash of civilizations thesis' mentioned in Chapters 2 and 4. In contrast to this discourse, Shannahan proposes an interpretative framework that emphasizes diversity as strength, intersectionality and a theology of creation that acknowledges and welcomes the superdiverse nature of our contexts and the growing engagement with dual heritage alongside the potential for strategies that emphasize a dialogical mutuality.[8]

Multiculturalism and 'Muslim Consciousness'

While multiculturalism in the British context has been strongly associated in public policy with race-relations legislation, the dynamics between race, ethnicity and religion in the development of the debate on multiculturalism are complex.[9] However, the development of what Meer has termed 'Muslim consciousness' as a call for recognition of Muslims as a minority group with rights and inclusion in an extension of race-relations legislation has been a significant factor in a critical drift away from multiculturalism by some previous advocates from the white liberal secular left and also the impetus for renewed criticism from long-term detractors from the political right. The centrality of Muslim identity to contemporary debates on multiculturalism cannot be underestimated and has brought religion into the centre of explorations of personal identity, communal rights and consciousness. Tariq Modood for a long time questioned the downplaying of ethnicity and religion by the anti-racist movement in the development of a political blackness that sought to unite the diverse communities who migrated from the former colonies into one political movement to resist prejudice and oppression. However, in communities of south Asian and Muslim heritage there has been a continued movement towards seeking recognition and struggling for rights on the basis of ethnicity and religion, with a concentration on the development of a stronger Muslim identity that may relate to Islam in a variety of ways not necessarily determined by religion. As Meer has pointed out:

> The relationship between Islam and a Muslim identity might be better conceived as instructive but not determining, something analogous to the relationship between the categorization of one's sex and one's gendered identity. That is to say, one may be biologically female or male in a narrow sense of the definition, but one may be a woman or man in multiple, overlapping and discontinuous ways – one's gender reflects something that emerges on a continuum that can be either (or both) internally defined or externally ascribed.[10]

Conversely, it is interesting that Meer has framed this developing 'Muslim consciousness'[11] within an understanding that draws heavily on the work of the anti-racist theorist W. E. B. Du Bois, and Richard Reddie has highlighted the role of Muslim consciousness among 'converts' of African-Caribbean heritage in affirming a form of black consciousness as a resistance to racism embedded in the dominant culture and Christianity's identification with that racism.[12]

Meer's analysis of a Du Boisian 'double consciousness' shows that it aims to reject both assimilation and separatism for a creative 'hyphenation'. Du Bois' strategy for promotion of African-American rights in a racist white culture was not to call for an 'over assertive' black nationalism or to plead for respect and assimilation but to live the tension of 'hyphenated' identity. Meer says: 'This is a kind of multiculturalism in which minorities espouse a hyphenated identity, contribute and participate equally but not necessarily uniformly. This would produce not only a better America but the "Better and truer self".'[13]

Meer then applies this analysis to how Muslims are perceived in Western culture and particularly in contemporary debates on multiculturalism where the emphasis is placed on Muslim communities to 'integrate' in a largely one-way process that misrecognizes Muslim consciousness as problematic rather than as a creative potential for the development of confident identities that contribute in their particularity to wider society in dialogue with others. Meer challenges negative portrayals of a more assertive Muslim identity by using detailed case studies to demonstrate the reasonableness, creativeness and complexities of the developing Muslim consciousness. He reverses the question about integration, directing it instead at Europe's inability to perceive Muslims as a legitimate constituent in Europe:

> At what cost will Muslim constituencies be denied a participatory space in the form of such things as provisions for Muslim schooling, discrimination legislation, and nonderogatory representation in mainstream public and media discourse? It is evident that there is a movement for some synthesis by Muslims themselves. Europe boasts a rich public sphere and a series of dynamic civil societies that have historically included and incorporated other religious minorities. The question with which it is currently wrestling concerns the extent to which it can accommodate Muslims in a manner that will allow them to reconcile their faith and citizenship commitments.[14]

Meer argues, drawing on wider theorists of multiculturalism, that self-consciousness exists only by being acknowledged and recognized, citing the Canadian multiculturalist theorist Charles Taylor: 'Non-recognition or misrecognition can inflict harm, can be a form of oppression, imprisoning some in a false, distorted, and reduced mode of being.'[15] The necessity therefore to affirm and recognize Muslim consciousness positively could be argued to be an important task for Christians seeking to challenge Islamophobia in themselves and wider society and to welcome our Muslim neighbour's contribution to enabling a move towards a healthy multicultural society.

Multiculturalism and Our Case Studies

We might consider how our three case studies in the previous chapter displayed tendencies towards one or more of Modood's categories of integration and Meer's ideas of Muslim consciousness. The Tower Hamlets case study appears to be the one most strongly embedded in a multiculturalist understanding. Alan Green's participation in the processes set up locally by the council and other local bodies following the Lawrence inquiry, and the multiculturalist impulse locally to extend this to the category of Islamophobia post the Runnymede Trust report, all display the dynamic identified by Singh, above, of local actions and coalitions being central. The role of the Interfaith Forum in that process and then in the response to the EDL highlights this. The central role of the diversely Islamic East London Mosque, over the more culturally Bangladeshi mosque in both the forum and leadership of resistance to the EDL, displays a developed multiculturalism and Muslim consciousness. Similarly, we are again minded to reflect on Green's identification of local Muslim youth as 'our' youth and the strong element within resistance to the EDL of whole community identification with the Muslim community, demonstrated in the slogan 'Whose Mosques? Our Mosques!' Islam in this movement in Tower Hamlets was not being seen as an 'other' but as an integral part of the community and affirmed in its Muslim consciousness.

In Bradford the women's response might be seen to display elements of cosmopolitanism. Certainly Clare MacLaren's scepticism of the religious leadership in the city and her distinction between 'devout and affiliated' and 'devout and unaffiliated' display sympathies towards an approach that has a suspicion of religious hierarchies and the potential for oppressive definitions of religion to dampen a creative engagement with the diversity present in the women's group. The informal Muslim–Christian spiritual dialogue that encouraged her, and led to a 'universal embrace', also reflects a more cosmopolitan approach, while echoing something of Meer's concern not to restrict definition of Muslim consciousness to strictly formal theological categories. Liz Firth's concern to avoid a faith huddle and engage with the diversity of Bradford beyond religious identity in an intercultural dialogue similarly sees the women's sympathies perhaps lying with some of the critiques of traditional civic multiculturalism that come from cosmopolitanism and sympathetic but critical versions of interculturalism.[16]

In Luton, however, the need for both Christians and Muslims to define themselves over and above violent groups within both traditions seeking to usurp the faiths for their own ends led to a strongly institutionally backed multiculturalism where the religious authorities in the town sought to describe and display a truer version of the faiths in their joint work for reconciliation and peace, which included a strong assertion of the need to engage and befriend Christian and Muslim acquaintances as your true neighbour, encouraging relationships at work and seeking to break down some of the geographical barriers in the town and move towards a two-way integration.

Each of our case studies could be seen to be engaging with the process of integration outlined by Modood, with varying degrees of multiculturalist and cosmopolitan sympathies.

Islamophobia as Resistance to Multiculturalism

While Modood and Meer critique Europe's difficulty in developing a multiculturalism able to positively include Muslim consciousness into contemporary society, Gabriele Marranci has argued even more strongly that far from being, as defined by the Runnymede Trust, an unfounded hostility to Islam, Islamophobia is:

> a phobia of multiculturalism and the transruptive effect that Islam can have in Europe and the West through transcultural processes . . . to create a multicultural society . . . it is not enough to allocate a space for the 'other', but also to accept the transformations that the cultural contacts and cultural interchanges with the 'other' may cause . . . Islamophobia today, is increasingly connected to the fear of a real multicultural society in which Islam may become a recognized and meaningful part of a new Europe.[17]

Marranci associates this fear of multiculturalism with the myth of Europe as a 'Christian monolithic entity' being lost through

Muslim migration. We might see here, as well as the obvious 'clash of civilizations' thesis, the vestiges of the Constantinianism that Yoder referred to (see Chapter 3). This requires then a further 'disavowal of Constantine' within Christian responses to Islamophobia. The dynamic between a form of disavowal and creative use of Christian and largely Anglican privilege in our three case studies is complex and the motivations for participation in tackling the EDL diverse. What may be required is to articulate more clearly a theological and biblical affirmation of diversity, therefore challenging monolithic understandings of 'Christian Europe' with a theological affirmation of plurality, diversity and multiculturalism rooted in the biblical narrative and open to learning from Islamic sources as a model of a theological dialogue willing to engage positively with Islam as a real, valued and continuing presence in our midst. This would be in the spirit of the analectic/kenotic process outlined in Chapter 2 that draws on the work of Enrique Dussel by challenging the totalizing myth of Christian Europe with an engagement with resources from Islam to enable and encourage positive readings of diversity in biblical narratives, and affirms Shannahan's hermeneutics of liberative difference.

Babel and Multiculturalism

One example of a suitable biblical passage to work with is the account in Genesis 11 of the tower of Babel. In this story we have the seeds of a theological response to multiculturalism and a challenge to perceiving Europe as a Christian monolithic entity. We have a story in which God creates diversity in the face of an attempted monolithic project of demonstration of power and control.

> Now the whole earth had one language and the same words. And as they migrated from the east, they came upon a plain in the land of Shinar and settled there. And they said to one another, 'Come, let us make bricks, and burn them thoroughly.'

And they had brick for stone, and bitumen for mortar. Then they said, 'Come, let us build ourselves a city, and a tower with its top in the heavens, and let us make a name for ourselves; otherwise we shall be scattered abroad upon the face of the whole earth.' The LORD came down to see the city and the tower, which mortals had built. And the LORD said, 'Look, they are one people, and they have all one language; and this is only the beginning of what they will do; nothing that they propose to do will now be impossible for them. Come, let us go down, and confuse their language there, so that they will not understand one another's speech.' So the LORD scattered them abroad from there over the face of all the earth, and they left off building the city. Therefore it was called Babel, because there the LORD confused the language of all the earth; and from there the LORD scattered them abroad over the face of all the earth. (Genesis 11.1–9)

In the story of the building of the tower of Babel, everything is ordered, there is a supposed unity of purpose. Everyone speaks the same language and decides that they should build a city together and have a tower that reaches up to heaven. But God is a jealous God and jealous of his authority, and he decides to undermine the plans of humanity who are apparently getting ideas above their station. As punishment he confuses their language and scatters them over all the earth. It is a story ripe for a hermeneutic of suspicion. Some questioning of the text seems appropriate. For a start, who wanted to build the city? Who did the actual building? I mean, who did the real work? Most importantly – as it is a question that arises out of the text's own concerns – why did they fear being scattered before the city was built? This supposed unity sounds a bit fragile to me! After asking the questions, in seeking the answers the story begins to look a little different.

Just maybe the universal language was imposed – one group imposing their language on others. Just maybe the apparent order was maintained by an oppressive regime and the tower built by slaves. Just maybe the fear of being scattered in the story is the fear of the oppressors that the oppressed will rise up against them, and their own awareness of the tenuous hold they have on power. In such a scenario the action of God in the story is to liberate difference – to give a voice to those who are not allowed to speak, who are unheard, who are not considered to exist other than for their use by the dominators who are telling the story. The oppressive singular grand narrative of the rulers is undermined. God's action is to bring otherness into the biblical narrative, creating difference and demolishing supposed order – an order of oppression. The tower builders' oppressive grand narrative of the way things are is demolished and local voices are liberated and flourish.

The story is often presented as if difference was God's punishment for the idolatry of building the tower that threatened, or at least failed to sufficiently recognize, the divine's jealous authority. However, this is the myth of those who lost their power. They perceive difference as bad, problematic, a result of turning away from God, whom they present to us as a jealous God. However, reading the story from the viewpoint of the silent ones who are given speech, the resulting pluralism is seen as liberation not curse. God confronts the tower builders of Babel, yes. For their idolatry, yes, not out of some vain fear for her power but because of the oppression and confinement that the rulers of this community put others under in order to 'make a name for themselves', as the story puts it.

We might want to read the development of multiculturalism and our current ethnic and religious diversity through the lens of this story, drawing on Dussel's work we mentioned in Chapter 2. Europe in the period of colonialism sought to colonize the world. The European imperialism, and the modern project with its roots in the conquistadors' 'conquering' of the Americas, soon after the removal of Islam from European soil, was a Babel-style project seeking to create a dominant monolithic European self-understanding rooted initially in an imperial or Constantinian view of Christianity. The reverse migration in the postcolonial contexts and the development of multiculturalism and increasing diversity within European societies[18] can be seen as a divinely inspired undermining of this monolith, and the call to Christians in this is, again, to disavow Constantine – in

the form of either imperial Christendom or Eurocentric colonial
modernity – and seek practices that affirm and embrace diversity, multiculturalism and, in the particularity of the development of Muslim consciousness, a spirituality that challenges
Islamophobia. Again, referring to our exploration in Chapter 2,
possibilities are created in this situation for an analectic process
that engages positively with the 'other' in our midst, to transform
Christian self-understanding through a positive engagement with
what Meer has called the rising Muslim consciousness.

Reading Babel Alongside the Qur'an

This interpretation of Babel, as affirming diversity as God-given,
can also be strengthened by an intertextual reading, drawing
it alongside Qur'anic texts that strongly affirm the God-given
nature of diversity. Asma Afsaruddin and others[19] have argued
strongly that traditional interpretations of Qur'an 49:13 and
5:48 affirm diversity and difference in ethnicity and religion as
God-given:

> O humankind! We have created you from a male and a female,
> and made you into nations and tribes, that you might get to
> know one another. The noblest of you in God's sight is the one
> who is most righteous. (49:13)

> For every one of you We have appointed a law and way of life.
> And if God had so willed, He could surely have made you all
> one single community, but (He willed it otherwise) in order to
> test you by means of what He has given you. So hasten to do
> good works! To God you all must return; and then He will
> make you truly understand all that on which you were inclined
> to differ. (5:48)

These passages could be read as affirming an engagement with
the multicultural diversity of our world and promoting a multiculturalist form of understanding of society that encourages

minority-group empowerment and two-way integration. The Qur'an also encourages a viewing of this diversity within an understanding of the oneness of reality. In Qur'an 4:1, Afsaruddin points out, we are told that human beings have been 'created of a single soul'. These two understandings of diversity and oneness are not a contradiction, she says:

> The theme of the oneness of humankind is repeated several times in the Qur'an. We are told that all human beings have been 'created of a single soul' (4:1) and that they are all descended from the same parents (49:13). At the same time, the Qur'an also recognizes and accepts the physical diversity of God's creation. This is not a contradiction; the Islamic worldview has often been described as based on diversity within unity, or 'the integration of multiplicity into Unity.' Within the global community of human beings who are equal before the Divine Being, linguistic, ethnic, and cultural differences are embraced as part of God's mercy. These differences are also projected as signs or miracles of God. 'And of His signs,' the Qur'an says, 'is the creation of the heavens and the earth and the diversity of your tongues and colours. Surely there are signs in this for the learned' (30:22). Diversity in physical appearance, ethnic and cultural traits, etc., is thus to be respected and celebrated as a desired feature of the divine design.[20]

Laying these texts alongside the Babel story strengthens a sense of God's affirmation of plurality and diversity and an understanding that encourages multiculturalism as a divinely ordained reality. Afsaruddin argues that interpretation of these texts falls into two categories: those arguing that the acceptance of diversity lies within the confines of institutional Islam and those in which the text points to a wider embrace of diversity beyond the confines of institutional Islam. She sees an embracing of the latter traditional interpretation as necessary for our times and an affirmation of cultural and religious pluralism.

Pentecost and Multiculturalism

In the old Anglican Alternative Service Book lectionary, the Babel story from Genesis was placed alongside the story of the empowering of the early Church with the Holy Spirit at the celebration of Pentecost, the intention being to show how Pentecost had reversed Babel, for now everyone heard about God in their own language and returned to a 'Oneness in the spirit of Christ'. This totalization of diversity within oneness mirrors the first of Afsaruddin's interpretations of the Qur'anic verses on diversity. However, contemporary Pentecostal theologians are concerned to develop a pneumatological theology of pluralism that does not want to quickly subsume the work of the Spirit under a form of totalizing Christological monism. Amos Yong has said:

> The strong and perhaps unmistakable inference to be drawn is that the preservation of the many tongues of the Day of Pentecost is an indication that God values not only linguistic diversity but also cultural plurality.[21]

As the account of Pentecost in the book of Acts says:

> When the day of Pentecost had come, they were all together in one place. And suddenly from heaven there came a sound like the rush of a violent wind, and it filled the entire house where they were sitting. Divided tongues, as of fire, appeared among them, and a tongue rested on each of them. All of them were filled with the Holy Spirit and began to speak in other languages, as the Spirit gave them ability.
>
> Now there were devout Jews from every nation under heaven living in Jerusalem. And at this sound the crowd gathered and was bewildered, because each one heard them speaking in the native language of each. Amazed and astonished, they asked, 'Are not all these who are speaking Galileans? And how is it that we hear, each of us, in our own native language? Parthians, Medes, Elamites, and residents of Mesopotamia, Judea and

Cappadocia, Pontus and Asia, Phrygia and Pamphylia, Egypt and the parts of Libya belonging to Cyrene, and visitors from Rome, both Jews and proselytes, Cretans and Arabs – in our own languages we hear them speaking about God's deeds of power'. All were amazed and perplexed, saying to one another, 'What does this mean?' (Acts 2.1–12)

After quoting Yong, the Nigerian Pentecostal theologian Nimi Wariboko goes further still:

> The event of multiple languages or many tongues that characterized the Day of Pentecost prioritizes a pneumatological approach to pluralism that invites us to honour multiple voices in discerning and solving problems of common social existence. This event cannot be interpreted as simply a diversity of tongues. In so far as the 120 disciples engaged in translation and communication (those observing them were no longer mere observers, but active participants in what is going on) there was an 'energetic engagement with diversity.' It was this kind of engagement that created the first church, 'the common society from all that plurality.' Luke does not just mention tongues, he takes time to name cultures that produced the tongues; I interpret this to mean that their identity, their differences, and angularities were worth noting and maintaining as they came into a common society not based on one essence but on each gift. The ethical implication for this is that at a minimum the participation of citizens in the public sphere should not entail the shirking of their religious and other commitments, but movement from there to context of plurality and active engagement with the diversity of other voices . . . in bridge-building dialogue for the sake of human flourishing.[22]

Such a reading of Pentecost takes what is normally read as a narrative for an affirmation of ecclesiological cultural diversity in a unity of Christ to a more publicly orientated pneumatology that reads Pentecost as an affirmation of cultural and religious diversity per se! The space for such similar generosity in traditional Qur'anic interpretation of 5:48 and 49:13 might be an additional impetus to encourage such a genuinely multicultural-ist interpretation that enables Christians to encourage a healthy and vibrant Islam in the European context as co-religionists and dialogue partners.

What resources are there within our traditions to enable such a movement and understanding?

Towards a Practical Theology of Multiculturalism

When the Prophet Muhammad began to receive the revelations that would become the Qur'an, they were not particularly wel-comed by the elites of the Meccan society, who saw them as a threat to their power. The revelations challenged the pagan prac-tices and questioned the rigid hierarchies of the society, as well as outrageous practices such as female infanticide. Muhammad was also attracting as followers many of the more vulnerable members of the Meccan society – the poor, women and slaves. As the elites of Mecca became more threatened, their dismissal and attack on the Muslims became greater, particularly on those more vulnerable members of the community, those unable to avail themselves of tribal links within the Meccan society that could protect them from persecution. It was in the face of this onslaught that Muhammad proposed that those who were most vulnerable to these attacks should emigrate to a place of safety. The place he suggested was Abyssinia, and the reason he sug-gested it was because he knew that there was a Christian king. Was it specifically because he was a Christian that Muhammad believed the refugees from Meccan oppression would receive a welcome and be granted refuge? This story is significant on many levels, but the focus I want to encourage for our context is how, in the face of persecution from pagans, it was to Christians that Muhammad first turned. And it is the level of trust he places in the Christian king, because he is Christian, that I think should speak to us today. Can we develop that level of trust among Muslims towards us as Christians, as Muhammad had for the Christian king of Abyssinia? Tom Wilson, in a recent work exploring Tariq Ramadan's call for Islamic reform,[23] argues, on the basis of Ramadan's use of this story, that it is not one to encourage dialogue. He cites Ramadan's reference to the Negus' later conversion to Islam.[24] However, Islamic tradition is not uniform in that opinion. Indeed, the earliest version of Ibn Ishaq's *Life of Muhammed* collected by Ibn Hisham has no record of the Negus' conversion, in comparison to Al-Tabari's later redaction of Ishaq, where a letter from the Prophet to the Negus calling for him to embrace Islam is recorded and the Negus' positive reply is also noted.[25] However, some have questioned the reliability of those later letters.[26] And there is a debate among Muslim scholars as to the understandings of this encounter.[27] Later sources on what the Prophet prayed on hearing of the Negus' death are also mixed: some say he prayed the full prayers said on the death of a Muslim; other sources say he offered prayers for the Negus on the basis that he was a righteous non-Muslim. There are also other arguments in favour of the continued Christian faith of the Negus. It is therefore with that second tradition that we identify this story, not as a defensive bulwark against the impact of the spirituality of the Qur'an on the Negus but as a resistance to the easy binaries of rejection and embrace framed in the language of conversion. The Negus clearly was touched and defended the beauty he discovered in Islam against resistance from his subjects, who were concerned that any acknowledgement of that beauty, even in difference, was giving ground. However, I would want to argue that the Negus was allowing the beauty to enhance while recognizing difference. If we seek to read the Negus' engagement with the Qur'an in this way, it provides a potential model for dialogical reflection on the story of Jesus' birth in Surah Maryam, particularly when set alongside Luke's birth narrative.

At the time of writing, a controversy has developed over the recitation of Surah Maryam at the Anglican Cathedral in Glasgow on The Feast of the Epiphany. Surah Maryam is of course particularly relevant to Christian–Muslim relations, not just because of the clear reference to Mary, the Virgin birth and Jesus. It was also the surah recited to the Negus of Abyssinia by the Muslim exiles seeking refuge with the king. This is the first institutional encounter between Christians and Muslims. The king recognized the beauty of the recitation while acknowledging clear differences. It appears appropriate, therefore, that the cathedral should also be a place to hear this surah when society is so full of Islamophobia and anti-Muslim hate. The Cathedral's actions demonstrate an appropriate radical welcome echoing the Negus' hospitality.

After hundreds of years of antagonistic relations between Christians and Muslims it is important to highlight this story as one among others that recounts the first major contact between Muslims and Christians, particularly at a time when Muslims face attack within the secular media. Can we become as church communities and as individual Christians places and people of refuge for Muslims from the onslaught of media-inspired Islamophobia and hatred, affirming 'Muslim consciousness' in the process?

The second resource for addressing Islamophobia is to meditate on Paul's words about love in 1 Corinthians 13. Although Paul is speaking to the context of the struggles within the Corinthian Christian community, the challenge he poses to the disputatious and divided Corinthian Christians can also be a challenge to us in our relationship with Muslims within the context of rising Islamophobia and anti-Muslim hatred. The primacy of love is the call to challenge ourselves, to look deep within our own hearts and allow ourselves to be convicted by the Holy Spirit of the fear and hatred that we carry for Muslims, to seek healing for this and become renewed in our minds and hearts, becoming truly countercultural in opening ourselves to positive relationships with our Muslim neighbours through practising Paul's manifesto of love. As Gordon Fee outlines:

> Paul is arguing for the absolute supremacy and necessity of love if one is to be a Christian at all . . . for without love one quite missed the point of being Christian in the first place . . . it is so tailored to the Corinthian situation . . . Nonetheless, as is often true of such lyrical moments this passage easily transcends that immediate situation as well, which is what gives it such universal appeal (if not universal obedience!).[28]

The call to love is a central scriptural challenge for Christian practice in our current context in relation to our Muslim neighbours. To quote Paul:

Love is patient; love is kind; love is not envious or boastful or arrogant or rude. It does not insist on its own way; it is not irritable or resentful; it does not rejoice in wrongdoing, but rejoices in the truth. It bears all things, believes all things, hopes all things, endures all things. (1 Corinthians 13.4–7)

Many evangelical groups have talked of the need to love Muslims as a counter to the other tendency within Christian evangelicalism to see Muslims as the enemy with whom we are in spiritual combat. However, although this approach is a welcome alternative to the negative antagonistic approach, it remains limited and still contains the agenda of seeking conversion and therefore prioritizing the 'wrong' in the other. My alternative understanding of Christian mission in this context is to apply Paul's 'Hymn to Love' to our relationships with Muslims in such a way as to witness to Christ through an open respect and love for those practices and presentations of Islam that speak to us of God's love. We will be witnessing to Christ's love by expressing genuine interest and openness to Islam and Muslims. We move through patience, kindness, challenging feelings of envy or arrogance in ourselves when we meet Muslims, avoiding resentment and irritability with practices we find confusing, different or challenging, and then through this process allow ourselves to begin to rejoice in the truth we find in Islam. In so doing we counter the concentration in the media on either falsely manufactured stories or a focus on minority or cultural practices we should and would condemn, and engage positively with growing 'Muslim consciousness' and encourage a healthy two-way integration multiculturalism.

In her book *The Im-Possibility of Interreligious Dialogue*, Catherine Cornille outlines the paradox in interreligious encounter: the discovery of both radical difference and common ground. The temptation, she maintains, is to stress one over the other rather than hold a creative tension between the two. She goes on to argue that in order to hold this creative tension positively, practitioners of faith traditions engaged in interreligious encounter need to develop the practice of five virtues: humility, commitment, interconnection, empathy and hospitality. These practices, she maintains, need to be resourced from within the practitioners' own faith tradition. She says:

> This book is neither an apology for dialogue, nor a glorification of the Christian role in it. It does not judge the truth of religions according to their capacity for dialogue. On the contrary, it recognizes the epistemic priority for believers of faith and revelation over any external demands or expectations. For this reason, it also proposes that if dialogue is to be possible, it must find its deepest reasons and motivations within the self-understanding of religious traditions themselves.[29]

My proposal is that the Hymn to Love in 1 Corinthians 13 is one such resource for Christians, and I argue that in practising the demands of the hymn, we both witness to our faith and practise Cornille's virtues, and also open ourselves to experiencing the same virtues within the practices of our Muslim neighbour, rooted in the particularity of their own tradition. In this process I link Cornille's five virtues to Paul's call to prioritize the practices that relate to the abiding truths inherent in living in faith, hope and love. This of itself requires humility and commitment, a recognition of interconnection and an openness built on empathy and hospitality.

> Love never ends. But as for prophecies, they will come to an end; as for tongues, they will cease; as for knowledge, it will come to an end. For we know only in part, and we prophesy only in part; but when the complete comes, the partial will come to an end. When I was a child, I spoke like a child, I thought like a child, I reasoned like a child; when I became an adult, I put an end to childish ways. For now we see in a mirror, dimly, but then we will see face to face. Now I know only in part; then I will know fully, even as I have been fully known. And now faith, hope and love abide, these three; and the greatest of these is love. (1 Corinthians 13.8–13)

Rejoicing in the Truth – Stories of Encounter

The following stories of encounter could be framed within a hermeneutic that seeks to concentrate, to use Paul's words, on a spiritual practice of 'rejoicing in the truth' that can be found in encounter with Islam rather than the usual practice of wider society in its Islamophobic response to Islam and Muslims, with its emphasis on 'wrongdoing' or to create stories that present negative images of Islam. They also welcome the contribution a 'Muslim consciousness' brings to society, whether it be the recitation of the Qur'an in a church at a time of war, the open practice of prayer in a hospital ward, the public recitation of the Adhan or the confidence of welcoming Christian newcomers into a community predominantly Muslim in makeup with Christmas presents and cards. In these stories the Hymn to Love is lived and the hospitality of the Negus is repeated, not so much in offering room in 'our' society for Islam but actually allowing Islamic spirituality to touch our hearts and transform us, allowing ourselves to be spiritually 'hosted' by our Muslim partners in dialogue. Each story is prefaced with a short quote that frames engagement with the narrative.

* * *

Doctrinal humility thus entails a certain degree of admission of the finite and limited ways in which the ultimate truth has been grasped and expressed within one's own religious teachings, practices and/or institutional forms.

Catherine Cornille[30]

It was after 9/11 and I was sitting with my friend the local Imam, Fateh Muhammad, among his books and papers in the little room where he slept, studied and welcomed visitors on the first floor of the house mosque that was at that time the place of worship and gathering for the local Muslim community in Hyde Park, Leeds. Fateh said to me gently: 'It is times like this that people turn to God.' And I knew he was right in a way; I had already been informed by members of my congregation that friends were

asking them if they could come to church with them on Sunday.
I asked him if he would come and be with us at our Sunday
Communion service that week and would he recite and trans-
late a passage of his choosing from the Qur'an. He agreed. And
at church that Sunday he beautifully recited from the Qur'an
and was a picture of gentleness, humility and love. The congregation – twice the usual size – were mesmerized by this image
of one who truly found peace in his heart through surrender to
God – the meaning of Islam. At the end of the service, in which
he gathered with us around the table as we broke bread, he said
to me: 'That was truly Christian – a beautiful service thank you.'
His openness and humility moved me deeply. The passage from
the Qur'an that he recited seemed so appropriate at the time,
from Surah Ta-Ha 1–8:

> We have not sent down the Qur'an to you to distress you
> but only as a counsel to those who stand in awe of God,
> a revelation from Him who created the earth and the high
> heavens;
> the Most Gracious is firmly established on the throne of
> authority.
> To Him belongs what is in the heavens and on the earth
> and all between them and all beneath the soil.
> Whether you pronounce the word aloud or not,
> truly, He knows what is secret and what is yet more hidden.
> God! there is no god but God!
> To Him belong the Most Beautiful Names

One day soon after I again turned up at the little mosque where
Fateh Muhammad was Imam to find him sweeping the stairs.
He greeted me warmly, laughing at my surprise at finding him
doing such a menial task. 'This is my jihad!' he exclaimed. Later
over sweet tea and fruit he spoke to me about the true meaning
of jihad. He told me of some words of Muhammad to his com-
panions on returning from a battle in the early days of Islam,
at a time when its very survival was threatened by aggressive
opposition in the Arabic world. Muhammad told them that they
had returned from the lesser jihad to the greater jihad, from the

physical battle in defence of Islam to the spiritual battle of the heart to surrender itself totally to God. This greater jihad, the struggle to surrender oneself to the mercy of God, is done, Fateh Muhammad said, through the cultivating of humility and compassion in striving against the forces of ego, pride, hate and greed. The Islamic scholar Hossein Nasr talks of this striving as the inner jihad residing in all the Five Pillars of Islam, and goes on to say:

> Through inner jihad, the spiritual person dies in this life in order to cease all dreaming, in order to awaken to that Reality which is the origin of all realities, in order to behold that Beauty of which all earthly beauty is but a pale reflection, in order to attain that Peace which all people seek but which can in fact be found only through this practice.[31]

* * *

Practise holy envy.

Krister Stendahl[32]

While studying Arabic, I made friends with three women on the course, all British-born, hijab-wearing Muslims of Pakistani and Bangladeshi heritage. I often found myself invited round for coffee, which would invariably turn into a full meal of delicious home-cooked food shared with the children; and knowing I was at one of their homes, the others would soon turn up to say hello, bringing more dishes, and children. They are inspiring women. Each has made an active decision to take on Islam as their way of life, wearing their hijab deliberately as a sign of commitment to their faith. How this way of life plays out in the domestic world of their lives is beautiful. When the baby cries somebody will rock her in loving arms and sing 'Allah' to her, or 'lââ ilâha illa–llâh', 'there is no God but Allah . . .' Posters hang on kitchen doors, with prayers to use for times of day, going to bed, preparing food, washing, going out – with every little action God is brought to mind. But I was always particularly struck by the way they manage the five-times-a-day prayers. It was not that prayer was an obligation and a nuisance interfering with the routine of the day, but a calling, a desire that they each understood, and in which they supported one another, so that each could prioritize her relationship with God, free from interruption. Each sister could simply trust her children to the others and claim those precious few minutes of solitude with God: 'You go and pray now, I'll watch the little ones . . .', and the baby would be passed from one sister to another, the little children played with, until mum came back.

I have never met a group of women who put prayer more prominently at the heart of their lives; I would have dearly loved this mutual support when my own son was little.[33]

* * *

The deepest level of communication is not communication but communion. It is wordless. It is beyond words, and it is beyond speech, and it is beyond concept.

Thomas Merton[34]

I woke to a familiar sound today. Even though the language was foreign, the voice unknown, there was no mistaking the sound of prayer. The Muslim daughter of the woman in the bed opposite was saying her prayers, her mother joining in, as and how she was able.

They included me into this small intimate circle and so I was able to meet with you in the company of friends, understanding for the first time ever, what speaking in tongues really means.

As the daughter prayed, it was obvious when she was using old familiar words, gifted words from saints long since passed. These she wrapped around us like a winter blanket, their undulating cadences being like the folds of a cloth she absent-mindedly rear-ranged so that they fell comfortably, snugly around us. I could hear the words of the Lord's prayer as she prayed her morning prayers and the words of the psalms as she recited her morning Surahs.

And when the familiar words had lulled us into warm, safe and secure spaces, she spoke from the heart – her words losing nothing of their rhythm, but now taking on an almost musical quality, a sweet lullaby for those she loved.

And you were there, and I heard and understood her prayer for me, for her mother, for herself, for the hospital staff and for the wider world; her language universal, even though her vocabulary was foreign to me.

She called you Allah, and I heard it as Abba – and I swear they were the same, for you were with us. And your gift of tongues enabled me to utter my Amen, in the space you made sacred beside a hospital bed.[35]

* * *

For me, prayer is a surge of the heart; it is a simple look turned toward Heaven, it is a cry of recognition and of love, embracing both trial and joy . . .

Thérèse of Lisieux[36]

In the Autumn of 2001, members of All Hallows Church in Leeds, where I was minister, joined with local Muslims to travel to London to protest against the bombing of Afghanistan in retaliation to the atrocity of 9/11. Church member Julie Greenan takes up the story and tells of the two experiences of prayer at the beginning and end of the march held in the middle of Ramadan:

100,000 people – two whole hours for them all to leave Hyde Park, where the peace march begins. Where the towering puppet figures were built: images of death and destruction, made of camouflage and webbing, with bayonets and machine guns for limbs, skeletal heads; collages of mayhem and chaos.

Near Speaker's Corner, one small group from one small church in one city stacks plastic boxes to form an altar. The rainbow altar cloth later becomes their banner. Ten metres away people following a different path unroll prayer mats and begin their prayers. The groups carry out their rituals alongside each other . . . Dusk in Trafalgar Square. Floodlit buildings of the British Empire. Beneath Nelson's Column, the muezzin sounds the Call to Prayer, before iftar, the breaking of the fast during the holy month of Ramadan. The fast that is kept in solidarity with those who have no food. The vast crowd stands in silence. At the breaking of the fast, bottles of water and dates are passed through the crowd. Food is offered in return, which is immediately shared with others. It is a colony of heaven . . .

I would remember that demonstration for weeks to come, especially the experience of the Eucharist, where our usual Sunday liturgy took on a new depth of meaning in the context of thousands gathering to resist the violence of war; the group of Muslims doing salah near us, the crowd of people who gathered around us, some joining in, others just observing silently, and then later the experience of the Adhan (Call to Prayer) before the prayers at the breaking of the fast. Increasingly at that time, I found myself reflecting on how the Call to Prayer had come to mean so much to me.

Allâhu Akbar Allâhu Akbar
(God is Greater! God is Greater!)
Allâhu Akbar Allâhu Akbar
(God is Greater! God is Greater!)
ash-hadu al-lââ ilâha illa-llâh
(I witness that there is no god but God)
ash-hadu al-lââ ilâha illa-llâh
(I witness that there is no god but God)
ash-hadu anna Muhammadan rasûlu-llâh
(I witness that Muhammad is the messenger of God)
ash-hadu anna Muhammadan rasûlu-llâh
(I witness that Muhammad is the messenger of God)
hayya 'ala-s-salâh
(Come to the prayer)
hayya 'ala-s-salâh
(Come to the prayer)
hayya 'ala-l-falâh
(Come to success)
hayya 'ala-l-falâh
(Come to success)
Allâhu Akbar Allâhu Akbar

(God is Greater! God is Greater!)
lââ ilâha illa-llâh
(There is no god but God)

When I look at the Call to Prayer in translation I long to stand with its bold statement against idolatry and its affirmation of the importance of prayer. But these simple words have a spiritual depth that is beyond their plain meaning and beyond questions about the status of Muhammad. I hear in it, as it is recited in Arabic, the truth of the human condition and the truth of our world – the wonder of creation and the painful realities of our wounds and our violence. The Adhan felt to me at this time like a beautiful mixture of pain and praise; and in Trafalgar Square on that demonstration it summed up the beauty of the Islamic path of faith, the beauty of the history of a land like Afghanistan and the pain of betrayal of a tradition by extremists, the pain of the oppression of a people by outsiders from Russia, the USA, Saudi Arabia.

* * *

Islamic extremists have created 'no-go' areas across Britain where it is too dangerous for non-Muslims to enter, one of the Church of England's most senior bishops warns today.

Daily Telegraph, 6 January 2008

It was our first Christmas in our new home. We had moved in the summer before (July 2009) into the area that is described as a 'Muslim majority area' and had settled in nicely, getting to know our immediate neighbours and others in the street. I was working on a sermon on Christmas Eve in the study for the Midnight Communion I was presiding and preaching at later that night, when there was a knock on the door. Luke, my step-son, answered the door and I heard him say 'Thank you very much' before closing it. 'Who was that?' I shouted. 'One of the little children from next door', he replied. 'He's brought round a card and a box of chocolates from his family and wished us a

Happy Christmas.' This happened twice more that evening as children from local Muslim families called round with a card and chocolates and wished us a Happy Christmas. Then a little later one of our Muslim neighbours appeared with some food – she thought we might be busy preparing for Christmas Day and might appreciate not having to cook that evening. Christmas in a 'no-go area' for Christians.

Notes

1 See for instance David Cameron's speech in February 2011, published in full at www.newstatesman.com/blogs/the-staggers/2011/02/terrorism-islam-ideology; or Ted Cantle's work in relation to Community Cohesion and Interculturalism – http://tedcantle.co.uk/publications/about-interculturalism; and also Trevor Philips, 'Race and Faith: The Deafening Silence', www.civitas.org.uk/content/files/Race-and-Faith.pdf. For a critical analysis of all these approaches, see Chris Shannahan, 'Zombie Multiculturalism Meets Liberative Difference: Searching for a New Discourse of Diversity', *Culture and Religion* 17:4 (2017), pp. 409–30.

2 See Marco Antonsich, 'Interculturalism versus Multiculturalism: The Cantle–Modood Debate', *Ethnicities* 16:3 (2016), pp. 470–93.

3 Modood has a substantial output of work and has been significant in addressing in articles and books the current critique of multiculturalism. His principal works include *Multicultural Politics: Racism, Ethnicity and Muslims in Britain* (Edinburgh: University of Edinburgh Press, 2007) and *Multiculturalism*, 2nd edn (Cambridge: Polity Press, 2013).

4 Gurharpal Singh, 'British Multiculturalism and Sikhs', *Sikh Formations* 1:2 (2005), pp. 157–73 (p. 170).

5 The argument presented in a collection of essays in the book edited by Hassan Mahamdallie, *Defending Multiculturalism: A Guide for the Movement* (London: Bookmarks, 2011).

6 Ali Rattansi, *Multiculturalism: A Very Short Introduction* (Oxford: Oxford University Press, 2011), p. 8.

7 Tariq Modood, 'Multiculturalism and Integration: Struggling with Confusions', in Mahamdallie (ed.), *Defending Multiculturalism*, pp. 64–6.

8 Chris Shannahan, *Voices from the Borderland: Re-Imagining Cross-Cultural Urban Theology in the Twenty-First Century* (London: Routledge, 2010), esp. ch. 11; and 'Zombie Multiculturalism meets Liberative Difference'.

9 A question mark could be placed over the category of 'race' itself because it implicitly assumes there are different essentialized human races rather than a single human race – see for instance Paul Gilroy, *Against*

Race: Imagining Political Culture beyond the Color Line (Cambridge, MA: Belknap Press, 2001).

10 Nasar Meer, 'Misrecognizing Muslim Consciousness in Europe', *Ethnicities* 12:2 (2012), pp. 178–96 (p. 189).

11 See Nasar Meer, *Citizenship, Identity and the Politics of Multiculturalism: The Rise of Muslim Consciousness* (Basingstoke: Palgrave Macmillan, 2010).

12 Richard S. Reddie, *Black Muslims in Britain: Why Are a Growing Number of Young Black People Converting to Islam?* (Oxford: Lion, 2009).

13 Meer, *Citizenship, Identity and the Politics of Multiculturalism*, p. 46.

14 Meer, 'Misrecognizing Muslim Consciousness', p. 193.

15 Charles Taylor, quoted in Meer, *Citizenship, Identity and the Politics of Multiculturalism*, p. 51.

16 See for instance the Conclusion in Rattansi, *Multiculturalism*.

17 Gabriele Marranci, 'Multiculturalism, Islam and the Clash of Civilizations Theory: Rethinking Islamophobia', *Culture and Religion* 5:1 (2004), pp. 105–17 (p. 116).

18 See for instance Steven Vertovec, 'Super-Diversity and Its Implications', *Ethnic and Racial Studies* 30:6 (2007), pp. 1024–54.

19 Asma Afsaruddin, 'Celebrating Pluralism and Dialogue: Qur'anic Perspectives', *Journal of Ecumenical Studies* 42:3 (2007), pp. 389–406.

20 Afsaruddin, 'Celebrating Pluralism and Dialogue', p. 394.

21 Amos Yong, *In the Days of Caesar: Pentecostalism and Political Theology* (Grand Rapids, MI: Eerdmans, 2010), p. 93.

22 Nimi Wariboko, *The Pentecostal Principle: Ethical Methodology in New Spirit* (Grand Rapids, MI: Eerdmans, 2012); Kindle Edition Location 1398.

23 Tom Wilson, *What Kind of Friendship? Christian Responses to Tariq Ramadan's Call for Reform within Islam* (Eugene, OR: Wipf & Stock, 2015).

24 Tariq Ramadan, *The Messenger: The Meanings of the Life of Muhammad* (London: Penguin, 2007), p. 62.

25 See Alfred Guillaume, *The Life of Muhammad: A Translation of Ibn Isḥāq's Sīrat rasūl Allāh* (London: Oxford University Press, 1955).

26 Karen Armstrong, *Muhammad: A Western Attempt to Understand Islam* (London: Gollancz, 1991), pp. 211–12.

27 I am grateful to two Muslim dialogue partners, Dr Dilwar Hussein of New Horizons in British Islam, and Sheikh Mohammed Amin-Evans of Birmingham, for highlighting the ambiguity in Islamic tradition on this story.

28 Gordon D. Fee, *The First Epistle to the Corinthians* (Grand Rapids, MI: Eerdmans, 1987), pp. 635–6.

29 Catherine Cornille, *The Im-Possibility of Interreligious Dialogue* (New York: Crossroad, 2008), p. 8.

30 Cornille, *Im-Possibility of Interreligious Dialogue*, p. 4.

31 Seyyed Hossein Nasr, *Traditional Islam in the Modern World* (Kegan Paul International, 1987), p. 3.

32 See Krister Stendahl's Three Rules of Religious Understanding at http://ancienthebrewpoetry.typepad.com/ancient_hebrew_poetry/2010/05 /krister-stendahls-three-rules-of-religious-understanding.html.

33 Story offered by Annie Heppenstall.

34 Thomas Merton, *The Asian Journal of Thomas Merton*, ed. Naomi Burton, Patrick Hart and James Laughlin (New York: New Directions, 1975), p. 308.

35 Story from the late Angela Shier-Jones.

36 Quoted in Thomas Ruhland, *Understanding the Catechism: Prayer* (Allen, TX: Resources for Christian Living, 1998), p. 8.

Index